UNDISTORTED GOD

RAY WADDLE

Undistorted GOD

RECLAIMING FAITH DESPITE THE CULTURAL NOISE

ABINGDON PRESS

NASHVILLE

UNDISTORTED GOD
RECLAIMING FAITH DESPITE THE CULTURAL NOISE

Library of Congress Cataloging-in-Publication Data has been requested.

ISBN 978-1-4267-6716-6

14 15 16 17 18 19 20 21 22 23—10 9 8 7 6 5 4 3 2 1
MANUFACTURED IN THE UNITED STATES OF AMERICA

To Alan

CONTENTS

INTRODUCTION:
A Decluttered Faith

There's a long and passionate spiritual tradition of waiting for God, waiting for revival, waiting for a personal sign or the end of time—waiting for something, *anything* to happen. But when the noise simmers down and the cameras stop rolling, another truth endures: God is waiting, the faith itself is waiting, patiently waiting out the world's false starts, waiting out my own inattention to the pulse of life. It's as if God is rooting for the soul to look, listen, brush past the distractions, get a move on, on toward the burning light, toward the divine presence, the indestructible news, a less distorted faith.

For years I was a daily journalist, a religion writer with a view of the great parade of faith sensations, the numinous and the non-starters, everyone's struggle to sift the real from the false. It was a great job, a continuous education. My desk in the newsroom was legendarily cluttered. I had trouble throwing away the slightest press release or the flimsiest new poll or study. Each scrap was a potential story. Surely it would all come in handy some day. Everything was a clue to the world's secret search on the ever-rising river of yearning.

But one can wade in the roaring current only so long. I eventually wearied of the late-breaking disputes of belief and my own relish for the battle. My interest was shifting. After nearly twenty years, I decided to quit the daily beat and clean out my desk's monumental mess. I was eager to pursue, move closer to, some divine impulse at the base of it all, some spark of permanence that survives the onslaughts of spiritual fashion and controversy. Maybe that spark could explain this great diversity of faith expression that we're all seeing today. Maybe it could fuse all opposites and misunderstandings and actually offer the "peace be with you" that people say to one another during church.

Religion has given civilization many traditions of intense inquiry and disciplined practice but also a littered scene of disunity and damage. The madness of bloodshed, so much of it religion-fueled, is a world crisis. I wanted to strip away as many false leads and pompous distortions as possible, including my own. Pay more personal attention to the force that has kept the writing going all these years: a tenacious sense that behind the furious search for spirit is a daily retrievable miracle,

> *I was eager to pursue, move closer to, some divine impulse at the base of it all, some spark of permanence that survives the onslaughts of spiritual fashion and controversy.*

the image of God imprinted on each of us, every moment carrying breakthrough potential and surprise and simplicity, a poem in the making, moving toward birth. Find that liberation and serenity: if possible, a decluttered faith, the search for God undistorted. "He strips the wind and gravel from my words," Robert Lowell wrote, "and speeds me naked on the single way."[1]

All this meant feeling my way back to the speechless fact of the Creator as well as the Jesus of record, catching up to them. That news, that poetry, that divine force, exists despite my fickle mood or the latest bad-news headline.

I admit my own religious receptors are just average, if not comically inadequate. As a churchgoer I'm often an underachiever. But bigger facts overshadow this or that detail: the moment-to-moment march of life's outrageous episodes and emotions—amazement, grief, hilarity, pain, transformation. In this freakish turbulence, signals do get through. In-breakings happen. They test the fabric of the familiar. They endure in the silence that returns after the noise passes. I've come to regard such moments as reminders of God, evidence of a divine persistence, the shadow and motion of the Creator. A divine presence. The divine *patience*.

There's no owner's manual or magic potion or quadratic equation to conjure it. But try to deny it or send it away or change the subject, and it still looms nearby, in Gospel reading, in the life of the senses, in music and prayer and memory and humor, in interactions with people, in the hard work of congregations, in tech revolutions and walks along the shore, in all the strange daily turns on the dance floor between mind and heart—whenever the soul itself stirs with urgency, looking for home, daring to dream dreams of reconciliation. People yearn to know it. It is restless to be known.

The secular world is pleased to ignore these matters or flatly contradict them. Every day, the materialistic dynamo grows louder, more confident, storming ahead by its own logic of money, ego, and extremism, throwing its elbows, eager to remove religious faith from the field of action.

The days are many when official religion indeed looks threatened—enfeebled and sidelined. The world of church, a moderating influence on society, gets outmuscled by the surliness of public life. People exclaim the divine name as much as a curse as a prayer. Society sings new hymns to the lone entrepreneurial ego or to utopias of the Internet. The telling of the divine story—a peacemaking venture in goodness and resilience—often dims in confidence or appeal.

Many believe this modern secular drift of things is inevitable. "It is what it is." This remarkable era of opportunity, exhilaration, and sensation is also known by other words, too—data glut, exhaustion, inequality, and rage, all shaped by haphazard economic, social, and spiritual conditions. Savagery creeps in, giving us a long war, an abusive economy, family dysfunction, political stalemate, financial misdeeds, delusional mass killings, secret addictions, and ornate conspiracy theories. These things deserve defiance, not compliance.

In such a day of extremes—not just the terrorist sort but extremes of media saturation, insomnia, wealth, poverty, glamour, boredom, and snark, not to mention weather—it's good to remember that extremes never get it right. They eventually collapse in self-defeat, excess, madness. They ignore or disdain the great sacred, self-evident truth that overshadows their schemes: existence itself is the shocking wonder. We can't account for the fact that we are here at all. Yet that fact solicits gratitude. We didn't have to be created. Yet we were—were launched on an adventure, where certain rules apply, and the outcome rides on our involvement. Everything points beyond itself. The meaning of the world is found outside the world.

I have no interest in writing a pious confession that panders to some in-crowd. I have no time for postmodern deconstructions of the living Christ. I'm wary of the narrowness of cold rationalism as well as the settled vocabulary of religious custom. Both sides—today's strenuous secularism and the welter of religious options—provide triumphant plot points in the tale of our contemporary spiritual era. Yet people are still left feeling cut off, lonely, shriveling, scared to death, angry as hell, flirting with evil, flailing with debt, losing sleep, their dreams blasted, frantic to start over, longing to discern their own voice against the noise, eager to fetch a spiritual realism to help them make the next move. The battle over what's real, what's permanent and undistorted and worth the fuss, is at fever pitch.

As an absent-minded baby boomer halfway home, I'm seeking a way out from under the chaos, tracing the glow and shadow of that first Easter morning that still haunts these scarcely believable days. Heaven knows (and my wife knows), clutter still hounds me. What's exciting is the endeavor of cutting a path out of it, by circling back to those strangely powerful, enduring materials of the faith, those sources of belief that fracture routine—moments of communion, eruptions of scripture, movements of soul, alignments of mind and body, encounters with the hidden image of God. Despite the darkness that's been done in the name of religion, there's a poetry to be pulled down from it that redeems the life around it, a poetry that's within the power of everyone, inciting the courage to think and to act.

I hope to share some odd turn or breakout moment toward gospel simplicity, confidence, defiance, relief, realism, or surprise—a return to foundations.

In every chapter here, I hope to share some odd turn or breakout moment toward gospel simplicity, confidence, defiance, relief, realism, or surprise—a return to foundations. I believe this circling back to inner sources—the access and undertow of antiquity, the silence of the spheres, the poetry of text or sky—is a way to clear space, to hear one's own name being called out on the road to truth and then move toward that beckoning. Removing all distortions in our perceptions of God is, of course, an impossibility. But a return to foundational astonishments can shake a person free of old habits and unexamined prejudices—distortions all. What happens then? A new journey commences, perhaps a less anxious one, a freer one. It's the work of a lifetime.

Jesus famously said his burden is light. That's always a surprising thing to hear from the teacher of hard sayings and redeemer of the world. Yet we should expect to keep looking for such surprises. Like those who populated the Gospels, we're all witnesses now.

Chapter 1

ELEMENTS OF GOD:
Wine of Astonishment

Something strange happened the other day. During a short worship service at our church, I went up for communion as usual, with my wife to my right. My head had been a swirl of useless, impatient thoughts far from the matter at hand: the body and blood of Jesus. The prayers had been said, and now it was time to approach the rail. Good—I was glad just to get up, get moving, and walk toward the altar, a sanctified stroll to escape the mental fog.

I waited on bent knees like so many times before. The minister leaned over to each person in turn, dispensing the little beige rounded wafers, heading closer, closer.

She skipped me.

My face froze. What just happened? Cool reason horned in: she's out of wafers, I thought. But no. She continued on to the others. I could see plenty of wafers in her hand.

Okay, theory two: she's mad at me. It was something I wrote for the local paper, where I was writing a regular column on the world of spiritual trends and religious debates. That stuff is finally catching up with me. She sent the column to a faraway committee of ecclesiastical oversight, where people in thick vestments are even now reviewing my status under God and suspending my liturgical privileges meanwhile.

I glanced at my wife, Lisa, who gave me a stricken look. I slowed my breathing to keep from panicking. Maybe the minister will reconsider. Maybe she'll double back and cut through all the red tape of a theological inquisition.

But this was embarrassing. Did others notice? Why does this sort of thing always happen to me? (Actually, this had never happened.) Now she came around with the wine. Some churches teach that taking just one of the elements has the same spiritual effect as taking two. So I'd settle happily for the blood.

She skipped me again.

This was serious. This felt like excommunication—a passive-aggressive twenty-first-century version. No formal accusation, no opportunity for defense, no confrontation at all, just a payback snub. My daily dispatches were dispatching me to hell. This suddenly made sense. Writing about the controversies of American religion week after week, who was I kidding? Not this church.

Everyone rose slowly from their kneeling spots and filed back to their seats. Should I stubbornly wait and force a showdown? My defiance lasted two seconds. I turned and trudged back to the pew, heavy, dreading. It was a confusing moment in this big house of God.

My head throbbed with the question: should I confront her in the receiving line? My wife, shier than me, shook her head with a grimace.

After the benediction, I approached the minister in the greeting line. I shrugged, smiled, looked a bit helpless.

"You skipped me up there."

Now she looked stricken, hand covering mouth. *Oh no!* she exclaimed. *An accident! First time ever!* She simply didn't see me. I quickly theorized that my blue blazer, in the half-light, caused a smudgy momentary blind spot in her busy ministerial eye.

People had dispersed, so she motioned to me to follow her right back to the altar. I kneeled again, and she handed me the wafer. I clutched it at last, then took the bare trace of wine from the chalice.

Now I felt fortified, back on track. But what on earth did that mean? I thought about the loaves-and-fishes fullness that four thousand people felt in the miracle story in Mark's Gospel. A few minutes before, I had known a subtraction. When the misunderstanding was corrected, I was part of the story again, the outlandish, world-bending story.

It all made me stop and think: What am I doing up here anyway? What's it about? Why bother?

Growing up, communion at church came around just once a month. One way you could tell communion day had arrived was by the decline in attendance that morning. Many didn't see the point of it. Communion was an interruption of the worship routine, so they quietly stayed home that week.

But I welcomed it. It got us out of our seats. I liked paying a call to the center of the action. It was a kind of inspection of a part of the sanctuary I never saw, up there in the sanctified zone where the preacher and choir stood. There were artistic details to get a close look at—the ceramic tiles, carpets, and stained glass, the carvings in the wooden altar table. And there we got to hold and taste those odd little pellet-like pieces of bread and take a bit of juice or wine. All this required bodily movement and blood circulation. It was our contribution to the service and a way to claim a larger piece of the sacred space. So I was glad of the interruption of routine. The routine wasn't enough for me.

Still, to explain what it meant to ingest the communion elements and make sense of the experience, to live by it, defend it, imagine life without it—well, I realized I needed to give a better accounting, to myself at least, of what's going on up there and why do it all these years and what difference does it make.

Now, after the communion rail derailment, I had reason to confront what it meant. I had to sit another minute. The slight aftertaste of wafer and wine lingered. It had weight. It was, at that moment, the only thing real about religion—not the doctrinal wars of words, not the PowerPoint messages from the pulpit, not my own dramatized distractions.

What was real was the way it connected me to the motions of a meal, the reconstruction of an ancient scene, a connective tissue across time. Imagination circles around this communion food and drink. It was plausible now to look up and sense the air still swirling in Jesus's wake, along with food he left behind, still fresh, the table only recently cleared. The world just carries on until he gets back.

In the last few minutes I realized: the truth proclaimed by the church is a vast moving force, and it neither depends on my unpredictable spiritual feelings nor conforms to my expectations of weekly worship as a cozy, reliable ritual affair. Yet I am free to join it, if I dare.

After church, we all stepped outside and scattered across the parking lot. We all faced a decision to leave the story behind or to take it with us. Now what? I had to get my bearings. If what's going on inside church is true, then what to say about all *this*—this golden sunlight, this seething asphalt life, this American empire, this afternoon's chores, this earth not of our making?

Out in the parking lot, I felt a shift in the interior tectonics. All week my head had been full of professional abstractions about spirituality in modern America—a narrative of existential strain and exuberance and controversy, the thousand-thread-count fabric of national religious debate, the raging retail economy of Jesus. For the moment now, all that was easing away. Under the boiling summer clouds and amid the cacophony of traffic, it had no use, no reach. The world was still there, but it was waiting to be rendered afresh, waiting to be noticed.

I could choose, in that post-Eucharistic moment, to keep walking the tight rope of commentary or to take the pulse of my own life. In that walk to the car, there was no GPS or app to arrange a shortcut through the risk of honest experience. I let those communion elements, prayers, and benediction unfurl in heart and mind. Something new was praying within me and trying to peer out.

After every worship time, once the Eucharistic table clears, the action shifts to us guests, who now become the hosts—the hosts of the Jesus story, the hosts of each other. The challenge is to be hospitable to what I'm now carrying, the elements and words ingested. It turns out to be more than a sip of wine or morsel of bread or fragment of prayer. It's the big picture and fine print, the whole story: something to live up to. It's my turn to be host.

It doesn't feel like a burden. A wooing commences. A door opens. The present moment becomes a staging area: a place for re-orienting contact with the imaginative life of God. Various words customarily apply—*grace, abundance, discipleship*—but what matters is the encounter with Jesus's words and what happens uniquely after, through listening and watching and moving forward. "Come and see," Jesus said in the Gospel of John to those first bewildered people who wondered what he was about.

Walking to the car that day, I reckoned this is no forced doctrinal march. Everyone has a choice to make about how and whether the Eucharistic experience matters. At the communion rail, I felt an absence, then a presence, a presence I can't quantify. The wandering Jesus figure keeps arriving, revealing a life more charged and less complicated, something worth trying to comprehend and move with, for the rest of my days. Post-communion, a confidence rises that says despair does not have the last word, and incessant conflict is not the main event. I acknowledge a little more solidarity with the travails of others. In the coordinated meal just finished, wherever it happens, the Son of God is reaching out to whoever is in front of him and whoever is in front of me. I'm amazed and glad, because like every-

That's the secret about religion: it better be worldly. Don't live it all in your head, doing the math of perfectionism. Don't forget the shaggy, swarming world.

body else I don't really have the time to do this just out of habit or just to go through the motions.

Now when I take the bread and wine, something catches in the throat: the yeast, the fermentation, the friction of life are in that contact. Jesus said to take it in remembrance of him. Remember blood, flesh, agony—the friction—but also the easy yoke, the turn toward a homecoming. That's the secret about religion: it better be worldly. Don't live it all in your head, doing the math of perfectionism. Don't forget the shaggy, swarming world. How odd that these modest materials of communion—a crust of bread, a swallow of wine—manage to contain the world, carry the grit of earth on their tiny surfaces. Anything could be an element. Anyone can be: the earth's seven billions, the forgotten, the famous, the famished, whoever's turning toward me or away.

That's a lot to remember. No wonder I need to take communion so regularly. "The world is the host," John Updike wrote. "It must be chewed."[1] Everything is in the bread and wine. Everyone is at stake.

Chapter 2

LARGESSE OF GOD:
Beyond iBelief

Some years ago I met a woman who took an especially keen interest in spiritual questions: What's the strangest religion I ever heard of, she asked me. How can anyone know which one is true? Big themes. It sounded like she was wrestling with a decision to go to seminary. Finally she told me what was really on her mind.

"I want to start my own religion," she declared.

She said it firmly, simply. I couldn't be sure she was serious. I waited for the punch line. None came. She continued: she had some ideas for starting a new faith that would improve on all the old ones. She figured there had to be something better than what the great world faiths offered, something spiritual, not religious.

That's when I realized: this wasn't a casual conversation. It was a professional consultation. I took a breath. I had already spent a long day interviewing a new minister in town and also researching the latest cult. I'd had enough of new religions. Maybe a little levity would help. I suggested that she'd need a solid business model to get her religion off the ground—congregational rituals, a well-rounded theology, focus-group feedback . . . and two or three thousand years of practice first. She didn't see the humor. I never saw her again.

This would not be the last such encounter with someone so ambitious. Over the years I've met several people who wanted to fashion their own faith blueprint, customize it, make sense of the world on their terms, cast off the useless parts of the big religious apparatus handed to them, and go solo. Their quest reverberates. The lone search for God or God's replacement—spiritual, not religious—is today an avocation, a battle flag, a credo of the yearning world.

Our conversation took place in a big Bible-belt Southern city, and, later, thinking about our talk, I tried to see the world as she did. Driving the streets, I watched the churches whizzing past on every corner, and at that moment they seemed to prove her point, looking like darkened museums, not shrines of living truth. Their sheer number appeared as an indictment, a testimony to redundancy.

That memorable discussion pointed to something that's hard for a churchgoer to admit: official Christian religion was losing touch with large ranks of spiritual seekers. It seemed to run at one speed only: slow motion. It stood accused of lethargic liturgy and used-up language. Then after 9/11, it got tarred by a newly inflamed chorus of atheists who said all religion was the enemy of humankind.

Somehow the coordinates of religion and belief—transformation, ethics, testimony, discipleship, divine presence—got knocked askew. The vocabulary lost traction. Taking a measure of their own spiritual potential, many people no longer turn to any church for clarity. In the new climate, it's possible to announce dreams of a new religion without apology or fear of ridicule.

There is no shortage of talk today at church-oriented seminars and conferences about villainous postmodernism, short attention spans, the tsunami of social media. But the questing self no longer trusts institutions that previously served as its partners. The adventure has moved elsewhere. To find hope or assurance or salvation, the self feels it must strike out on its own.

This new condition—this magnification of the self—puts a lot of pressure on the self. There's a hidden anxiety about carrying such a burden. But the self has enablers and co-conspirators. One of them is the ideology of individualism.

It's not easy to question individualism. One of its tricky traits is that it's nearly impossible to criticize it without looking unpatriotic. Individualism is in the DNA of the USA. It's an essential ingredient in the nation's dynamism. But the old checks and balances—the self's dance with community, tradition, respect for the past—have lost their check and their balance.

Previously, the self had been one player among many. There was interplay with congregation, civic club, neighborhood, and elders. But society has shifted, ceding muscle and weight to the individual, the self. Individualism has become fiercer, bolder. Somewhere along the line, back in the 1970s (or maybe the 1770s or the 1570s), the culture's voice shifted from "we" to "me."

"Our mission is you!" the gym brochure tells me. "There's only one you!" the supermarket placard assures me. Even Freud is in decline—Freud, who warned us that life is a problem and we must learn to mind and mine our neuroses, name and subdue them, keep them in check. The eclipse, in my lifetime, of the Freudian idea as an explanation and solution to the self's problems is no less shocking than the fall of the Berlin Wall.

Entrepreneurial and buoyant, the self seems to have entered a new golden age of sovereignty. Other solitary selves take in the news, too, and initiate their own private coronations by the billions.

But monarchy is high-maintenance work. The self's care and feeding requires more and more, a bigger canvas and echo chamber for its devouring freedom. Its logic is ruthless and perfectionist and easily bored.

I feel it. I feel this climate working on me. It daily offers a million options—technological, consumer, social-sexual. I feel the power of choice, a growing impression that I don't need help from anyone else to find excitement and sensation. Every morning I wake up to a world that feels a bit more accommodating to the self's demands, a little more hollowed out and gnawed away, than the day before. I've got a smartphone and a laptop that open on a trillion other screen-delivered worlds. What else could a person want?

Counterweights still exist—team sports, concerts, school boards, national elections, congregations. These remind me that I'm not alone and can't do everything alone. Yet they start looking like leftovers from yesteryear. Society seems to be hurtling forward in an experiment devoid of community elements. The times they are a-feverish, exciting, uncharted.

And that's when I know it's time—time to breathe deeply and say a prayer. Bow the head and return to earth. Time to guide the high-flying self into the waiting dark, eyes closed, turning to face in the direction of the greatest unknown.

Here I am, unplugged and unimpressive. Help me wake up. Keep me alert to my real tasks and to the presence of other people. Amen.

I have no expertise at prayer. I cannot give advice. All I know is: prayer, no matter how clumsy, reminds me that something greater is at stake than my inadequate piety or lack of polished words or any over-baked commentary on a changing culture. Something greater stands nearby, closer than close, a presence that deserves attention.

At the moment I'm not even using the name *God*. Everybody knows the suspicions about prayer—that it's a one-way chatter into the void, no one listening at the other end. But anyone who prays pushes ahead, even if they have to carry the baggage of their every doubt. I am often changed in the act of it.

For one thing, I am exposed: my vague, buffoonish rhetoric stands in need of instruction, in need of a spirit of trust. To my surprise, the exposé isn't embarrassing. It's a relief. The unnamable presence regards the scene, waits, suspends judgment. The steady, unblinking presence becomes a Presence: somehow it teaches, even blesses, and I am returned to the light of day. That's a lot for Nothing or No One to be doing.

There's something sensible about this low-tech capacity for unedited prayer. The self, attempting to pray, enters a clearing, a benign emptiness, a zone of mercy, a frontier of freedom,

> *I have no expertise at prayer. All I know is: prayer, no matter how clumsy, reminds me that something greater is at stake than my inadequate piety or lack of polished words or any over-baked commentary on a changing culture.*

sponsored by something other than the self. There's an invitation to make oneself at home. The alternative—say, a blinding divine light, an overwhelming visitation—wouldn't allow me a second to think my own thoughts. The divine Presence withdraws part way to allow us our own space.

Even when prayer is most private and tentative, I think of it as joining a vast caravan, a conclave, a conversation. That's what religion is: the individual's long conversation with long-hovering forces outside itself, as well as a power deep inside, accompanied by other individuals with their own similarly stuttering contributions to make.

Taken this way, a decluttered biblical faith reaches for just two or three basic ideas:

One: God is Creator. We're not.

Two: the needed news comes from outside oneself. The ego is too flawed and blind to provide completeness on its own.

Three: hearing the news requires a pragmatic openness to experience, a sense of proportion and modesty, because the next bulletin or epiphany might come from an unlikely source—a person approaching from across the hill or a disheveled manger or an empty tomb.

All this requires a skepticism about conventional wisdom. Yes, skepticism. Belief in God implies a critique of human pretensions that secular optimism misses. Monotheism is a rebuke to excessive self-regard, hubris, and overreaching. It lets the self know where the self stands: only God is God, so let's drop the stagey swagger and petulance. Belief in God names and indicts the violence festering inside. Belief is something intensely practical and unsentimental.

It's tempting to think the self is powerful enough to reconceive the world every day, redesign God and religion. The self talks a good game, but does it really know what it wants? It keeps changing its mind. So do the signs of the times. The moment is fluid, impermanent. The dynamo of change surges impulsively on.

Religious tradition meanwhile carries on despite all the sociological predictions of its demise. It's here to keep supplying the self with arguments to chew on, reasons to slow down the self's racing brain and to enlarge the menu of ideas. Facing the strange and outlandish news of belief, the individual might discover a new quest: the freedom to explore it, argue with it, test its claims, investigate its history and endurance, or even find a spot within it, moving it forward, becoming a witness, coming into one's inheritance as a working poet of the image of God. Otherwise the self forages on its own, at times tasting the poison mushroom, thinking it's on a heroic sojourn that no one has attempted before.

I don't know whatever happened to my distracted spiritual-voyager acquaintance, whether she succeeded in starting a new redemption story on her own or simply joined most of the rest of us in the endeavor to link up with something larger than ourselves. I hope she found a wide-berth place that's generous enough to include newcomers who toy with dreams of the self but secretly want a place of rest, a place of truth.

Chapter 3

SON OF GOD:
Go Crazy

I was standing in line at a bank on a Friday, with its mix of payday high spirits and savings account anxiety. This branch office was but a tiny suburban node of the crackling nervous system of world markets, money exchanges, and rumors of collapse. The drama was playing out here, too, the human condition in all its broken-down splendor.

In front of me stood an exhausted brick mason; behind me, a bony self-conscious young woman. Off to the side was a shy young Mexican family of three, waiting for the bank manager here in a foreign place, waiting with incomprehensible patience.

I stood in line and fretted: too much time to think about insufficient funds, stingy CD interest rates, possible robbers busting in, the unstoppable soft rock piped in to sooth us wary patrons.

And that's when I heard, through the bank lobby speakers, James Taylor's "Fire and Rain," in which he asks Jesus to look down upon him and help him make a stand.

It came as a blast from the early 1970s, a mostly dead zone between the Beatles' breakup and the advent of the Clash. Into this void sang Sweet Baby James, no Jesus freak: this was the first reference to Jesus I ever heard in a pop song (this was just before *Jesus Christ Superstar* and *Godspell*). It was startling. Taylor was making a prayerful plea for divine aid. Look down, Jesus, from your elsewhere perch, and please do something.

I perked up in the bank line at Taylor's Jesus moment. Strange to hear *Jesus* in the sober-solemn all-business interior of a bank, the blessed name stripped of Sunday ritual packaging. Yet, as the Gospels imply it, this is more or less how the first disciples heard about it—at work, out in the marketplace, at the drive-through, at the shoreline, in places beyond the walls of official religious life.

In the bank, no one was paying attention. By now, invocations of the sacred name are blandly familiar. Everybody exclaims Jesus, ready to put him to work on some scheme. "Jesus Christ!" the stand-up guy says on Comedy Central to get a cheap laugh. Or, "Jesus!" I gasped last week when I saw the news that two hundred more people were instantly blown up in Afghanistan. I said it again last night when an SUV almost ran me over. I imagine Jesus looking up expectantly from his Father's business every time he hears this, then turning puzzled and disappointed yet again at human thoughtlessness, this world's parade of reckless words and actions.

At least James Taylor's approach to Jesus, despite the song's smash-hit pop-40 status, sounded humble, a plea from a place of weakness. He's asking, not assuming.

This offered me a little moment of clarity in the bank line, a brief break from the contemporary Jesus condition. We have a strange way of loving the savior. We're a culture of competing Christs, a world of jostling Jesuses. Everyone claims a user-friendly redeemer to shore up a particular vision of holiness or political prejudice. It's embarrassing. Who is Jesus? I could name thirty different Jesuses right now—or is it three hundred? Or three hundred million?

Each one—the Jesus inside our heads—claims a niche in the bullish religious market. Here are seven, which might say more about today's passing moods and dreams than about a Galilean walking the earth two thousand years ago:

- Free-market Messiah. This Jesus gives a thumbs-up to global capitalism and frowns upon international efforts at world peace (the United Nations). The sermon about Love Your Enemy isn't in the publicity packet.
- Peace-and-Justice Jesus. This rebellious leftist sage topples the status quo and exalts community solutions. His healing miracles get passed over. So do his own words about returning in a storm of tribulation.
- Silence of the Lamb (of God). This is the Christ of the scholar-skeptics who doubt what scripture attributes to him. He's a mystery. They ignore another mystery: how people came to worship such a mystery.
- Rapturous redeemer. This is the Jesus of armageddonists who conclude Satan has more power than God in this world. The Second Coming is our only hope.
- Self-help holy man. Positive-thinking bestsellers describe an upbeat God-man who helps those who help themselves in a status-quo society where workaholism and overspending coexist unchallenged.

- Childhood Christ. Not his childhood—ours. This is the Christ of early memories, whether gentle savior or high-strung judge, depending on what was preached week after week—the faith one now recalls, or rejects, in turbulent adulthood.
- Gnostic prankster. This is a defining Jesus of the last decade, the wandering guru who uttered oddball aphorisms, married the Magdalene, and suffered death by church distortion.

Amid all the versions of Jesus on the spiritual map, I notice one thing: Jesus doesn't get to speak. He is seldom quoted and never at length. His words in the Gospels—the Sermon on the Mount, the Lord's Prayer, the many parables—are the closest thing we have to a historical record. Yes, we know scholarly argument has cast centuries of doubt on the historical accuracy of New Testament writings, but I suspect there's another reason for the resistance and neglect: not that there's too little reality there, but too much of it to handle.

In the Bible, Jesus's words are a mix of welcome and difficulty, grace and trouble. He is too intense and unpredictable to belong to any clique—whether in first-century Holy Land or a twenty-first-century political lobby. In the four Gospels, Jesus blesses the peacemakers but also brings a sword of judgment. He beckons the

In the Bible, Jesus's words are a mix of welcome and difficulty, grace and trouble.

little children and heals the sick but impatiently dismisses family feeling. He seems to mean a hundred things at once. Love God, fear God, show mercy, be righteous, live the Golden Rule, expect the fiery Reign of God from heaven, and look for it also inside the heart.

The tension between these different motions builds and builds. The paradoxes, for many readers and believers, become too unbearable to hold together. The stress-reducing temptation is to fall to one side or another, to pick only one flaming theme and run with it.

But the point is to hold them all together somehow—because the Gospels do. We were given one Jesus, not two or two hundred according to whim. This Gospel Jesus contradicts the multitudinous Christs of commerce and culture war that urge me to hate the enemy across the seas, across town, across the aisle.

So I read the Gospels to keep from going crazy.

In the Gospels the reader is suddenly dropped into a wild-weather high-stakes plot, with the cast of characters thrown off course by the news and deciding to join in or stay off-camera. The Gospels keep Jesus on a line of sight. They map the outlines of a life—teacher, rabbi, healer, Son of Man, Son of God, purveyor and surveyor of the Kingdom of God, the news pouring onto a battered planet. Reading the Gospels, I find Jesus there in the corner of my eye, swift-moving, a mind and body speaking or not speaking, coming in fast.

There are of course shelves and shelves of book-length studies of Jesus, yet nothing is ever settled. The Gospel writers understood that nothing in real life—in the ministry of Jesus, or in our own passing, piled-up days—is as neat and linear as a scholarly presentation. The four Gospels unfold in small units, sections, like scenes spliced together, as if that's how it felt—feels—to experience him. His every episode released something new—each glance, initiative, and decision. He looked up in the trees to find people hiding there. He spoke at crucial moments—witty or withering. Sometimes he dared to say nothing at all, instead crouching silently in the dirt while others bickered. What he was doing was often disruptive or startling, impossible to see in a big-picture scheme. For the witnesses, what counted was what was happening on the ground before their eyes, each moment with him. That's what they remembered. That's what overwhelmed them, those bursts of light, returning them to some startling information—the Reign of God around the corner, the image of God within, the awareness of God in reach. He showed them what it looks like and feels like.

Matthew, Mark, Luke, John. I return to Mark most of all. It's the shortest, the most economical account of Jesus. It is jarring, terse, action-oriented, cinematic, strange. It has a laser-like focus, with much on its mind. To read Mark is to return to the Jesus who is the subverter of easy assumptions about him.

Mark practically invented the form of the Gospel. From the opening verses, Jesus steps into view out of nowhere and never stops. This Gospel, written around 65 CE, was a freshly cobbled form of writing busting out of the ancient world's dusty horizons. The old wineskins—ancient biography, mythology, epic, epistle— couldn't quite contain the story. This genre was different, created perhaps out of impatience. The writer was a man probably sitting in Rome, probably a friend of Peter, fashioning a record of events. The tale had been circulating for three decades, but now the writer of Mark would transfer it to papyrus so the faith could rise yet again with every new audience.

The Word made flesh—now the Flesh made word. Transferred from word-of-mouth to words-on-paper or screen, the Gospel became something bigger: a new tabernacle, a portable portal into heavenly business. Reading Jesus became a new way to know him and affix him to the heart. To read the Gospels was to watch the whole Jesus story march before one's eyes—the Real Presence, offered on the page in a trinity of past, present, and future.

Mark's Gospel, likely the oldest, the closest to the scene, is curiously passed over in our keen latter-day attention to overlooked Gospels lost or gnostic. The Gospel of Mark is the real lost Gospel. Its brevity, rough edges, and lack of slickness are a scandal to modern style. Mark swoops in, the great declutterer, the silencer of that crowded bullpen of messiah complexes. He calms the distortion. I read Mark with great relief.

Facing the edgy paradoxes of the Gospel texts full-on is an alternative to mere picking and choosing and soft-pedaling the troublesome spots. I believe there's a physiology of faith: the act of reading and rereading scripture sinks slowly into the bones. The words come to inhabit the body, despite the disharmonies. The body of Christ is a mystical idea, but also a practical one: the body of Christ is each believer carrying around the Word on earth, the Bible's story of creation, fall, and redemption. A transfer is made from page to eye to heart, blood stream, and muscle lining. This makes belief a matter of embodiment—getting the body moving in certain directions, catching the current of the Gospel stream. It's a matter of action, not a matter of reciting certain biblical catchphrases in a certain order to prove club membership. Reading opens on inwardness, which then turns outward.

You might protest that the New Testament falsifies or freeze-dries the many fluid early-church attitudes about him. But there was one solid person roaming Judea, not a confluence of shadows and rumors. Whoever he was, he is revealed in the reader's long encounter with sources that have survived the test of two thousand years. He finally eludes every impulse of the zeitgeist, every itchy reduction. The sacred text captures a moving picture of Jesus, which is always heading this way in real time, whether the pop songs are piped in or not.

Chapter 4

REBIRTH OF GOD:
Verb and Reverb

The scene was Las Vegas, a Jesus parade in 110-degree heat—a squadron of Christian evangelists marching through the streets, past the vast casinos, making protest against the fleshpots and gambling dens of the western American desert. I was reporting it on deadline.

The early afternoon light was bleached and blinding. The sturdy-souled marchers refused to wilt. Few people lined the streets to watch. In the baking heat, there were more paraders than witnesses. This only deepened the marchers' determination. The inconvenient conditions, the lack of spectators, the lack of gratitude for their exertions all confirmed to the evangelists the hard truth of the narrow way, the rigors of the spiritual war at hand. All this gave the marchers vigor and purpose. And anger.

I trotted along, no hat or sunblock, dutifully covering this unusual demonstration for my newspaper back home. I tried a few respectful, boilerplate questions.

"What do you hope for the people of Las Vegas?" I asked one of the marchers, a minister. "Do you think the parade will make a difference in people's lives?"

He turned on me, who suddenly served as a handy denizen of the secular media.

"Are *you* a Christian?" he demanded. "Where do you go to church?"

I mentioned something about an Episcopal congregation.

"Let me tell you something. If that's where you go to church, you're no Christian. When were you saved? You don't know, do you? You're no Christian if you can't tell me the day, the hour, and the minute you were born again."

I had to decide whether to escalate the discussion or just stay composed in this desert apocalypse, keep scrawling my notes and file the feature story about a small army of robust Protestant evangelical protesters in the city of sin.

I stuck with reporting. But I've since wondered at his bristling assumptions about faith and damnation and how quickly our little exchange turned into an arid canyon of broken communication between two ostensible believers.

He had his story of salvation, and he was sticking with it. And I have mine.

A friend later said I should have fired back at him that I know exactly when I was saved: it was two thousand years ago, when Jesus died on the cross. I never was good at snappy comebacks.

The churches I grew up in never talked about salvation as a lightning-bolt moment of transfiguration. They were wary of the emotional theatrics that can attach to such scenarios, the temptation to turn a private mystery into a canned and tearful prime-time retelling. The churches I know focused instead on the long haul of belief—opening up to the Jesus story now and over a lifetime, allowing his teachings and his spirit to inhabit the heart, becoming a member of the body of Christ, trusting Providence on the many turns along the way, weighing the demands of discipleship, focusing on Golden Rule ethics more than doctrinal niceties flamboyantly defended. In the reigning spiritual marketplace, this approach is apparently considered a bore, a strategic failure. I suspect that's what my church liked about it: better off with an unglamorous story of quiet or stammering commitment, and not be competitive about it.

Accordingly, in the 110-degree heat on the burning Vegas asphalt, I could have listed an unwieldy number of personal moments when the faith shyly or slyly came calling. Call them wake-ups, doors ajar, or divine turning points—the April morning I was baptized (at age six months), the day the church gave me my first Bible (Revised Standard Version, age thirteen), the week I felt the strength of church community on a mission trip (New Mexico, age seventeen), the moment I finally got it that the Resurrection happened somehow in real history and I must reckon with it (Easter sunrise, age twenty-five), the moment I really beheld the Ten Commandments and the Sermon on the Mount as foundational truths of human sanity and purpose (age thirty), the moment I realized the indispensability of prayer (age fifty). But no ponderous rehearsal of my "spiritual growth" would have impressed my sun-burned accuser.

That's a tragedy of modern Christianity—the long-nurtured, closely guarded sectarian divisions between believers over the credentials of one's conversion, even the style of telling the story of one's redemption. But never mind. There are many ways to tell the tale, many ways through to the other side.

Poet Muriel Rukeyser once wrote that "the universe is made of stories, not of atoms."[1] Atomic scientists will disagree, yet then they go right off and tell the latest theory, the latest story, about the nature of the universe.

Each year, I teach a writing course, and by day three we talk about the two-story theory. According to this often-quoted idea, there are really only two stories in the world:

One begins, "A person sets off on a journey . . ."

The other starts, "A stranger walks into town . . ."

In a pinch you could pour the world's religions into one of these story molds or the other. In the book of Genesis, Abraham and Sarah set off on a journey. So does Noah and his family. Later in the Bible, so do Mary and Joseph.

Then comes the figure of Jesus, the stranger who walks into town . . . who invites everyone within earshot to set out on a journey with him.

The life of everyone on earth finds itself moving between these two stories—sometimes you're the stranger, other times the journeyer, sometimes both at the same time. Whenever you set out for a new city or job or circumstance, you are also the stranger wandering into town, poised at the crossroads of uncertainty and potential. Everyone is in on the equation. We're all in this together.

In class, though, younger students usually protest the two-story theory: they don't want to be limited to a choice of two stories in life! They want a bigger menu. They will not be constrained by this arbitrary math. They're just starting out and want to mint their own new narrative.

Fair enough. It will be up to them to discover what kind of story they'll shape out of the gleaming challenges that await. Some day they might reach the same tentative, reassuring conclusion I have: life on earth, a complicated affair, can be boiled down to a few structural simplicities after all. I tell them to get back to me in about forty years.

Yet here's another wrinkle: even the endearing two-story idea might be trumped by something simpler, something larger: we are all roaming around inside the One Big Story.

It's difficult to see amid life's torrent of data and perils. But a grand drama still barrels along across time—whether we are paying attention or not, whether our times can hear it or not. It's a drama caught by the biblical texts—a story that gave people a trust in the universe despite every tragedy. The ancestral, providential story line defies political discouragements and cruelties. It gives people a sense of proportion. Generations incessantly debate the Bible's details, genres, and meanings, but I refuse to lose sight of scripture's essential, unwavering big-picture narrative message: the Creator of the universe somehow oversees and attends to human history and delivers ethical signposts—the teachings of patriarchs and prophets, Jesus's life and resurrection, the promptings of conscience. Everything points to clumsy humanity's search for God, or is it God's search for us?

I love the quote from Jewish writer Isaac Bashevis Singer: "God is a writer, and we are both the heroes and the readers."

I love the quote from Jewish writer Isaac Bashevis Singer: "God is a writer, and we are both the heroes and the readers."[2] It's rare to see a theology delivered in thirteen words. His words imply a narrative to this life, a narration perhaps still being written. Possibly it's still in rough draft. But the narrator, a writer—the Creator—is at work (working on deadline?). And it suggests there's a plot, with a beginning, middle, and end (preferably in that order). It sounds paradoxical to be both the readers and the heroes. But one without the other won't do. It would put a person out of balance. A life of strict reading would cut itself off from life's material demands and opportunities. A life of heroism stripped of thought and interpretation sounds like action without purpose.

The image of God as author echoes the famous theme announced in the Gospel of John: "In the beginning was the Word." Not breath or voice or idea or demand or doctrine or binary number or screen, but word. In Genesis, God uttered words to create order and stay the chaos.

"In the beginning was the Word . . ." The vibration of that original act—not big bang, but first verb, and now the reverb, the reverberation—lives on. It is living out in everybody.

All storytelling is a remnant of that original diction. To be made in God's image means we have retained the storytelling instinct, the power to take the reader on a voyage, defy the chaos, deploy poetry and resolve.

Those things require clarity of mind and courage. In short, they require heroes. There's nobody around but us to tell the story and try to do right by it.

The born-again narrative is one way. To those who experience transformation in that fashion, it is the only way to get the story told. Problems arise if "born again" becomes code for an ideology of exclusion. It starts to look like an eagerness to build a certain kind of house of faith—airtight and safe from intruders. The compulsion expands so that every house in the neighborhood should look like this one. It becomes the town standard. Other styles are unwelcome.

There's another way. Claim one's place in the hurtling processional of creation. Ride the wave that began at the very beginning and includes each of us in our own time and asks for a response, a yes. Under the circumstances, despite a thousand unanswered questions, it seems ungrateful to say no.

"If Christ were born within my heart, He would no longer have to roam the earth an outcast, alien by birth."[3] With that line, Angelus Silesius, a seventeenth-century mystic poet, upends some cherished mental habits. Silesius's metaphor turns an all-consuming argument about spiritual credibility upside down: belief is not about precise timetables of conversion or the minutiae of my religious resume. It's about altering the conditions of practical life so the gospel can find a place to land. A preoccupation with the hydraulics of one's own rebirth gives way to a bigger idea: Jesus reborn in human beings. If Jesus would be "born again" on earth, then it's up to people to step in as midwives, prepare to take action, and see the fragile new beginning through. A minute ago I was a harried passerby, busily calculating my own spiritual blood count—but now enlisted as an attendant who is called on to help deliver a savior into the unsuspecting world.

Silesius's words could provide a healing moment among divided believers. It's a way to talk about transformation without retreating to battle stations and hostile jargon. There are no enemies in this. The power of metaphor—Jesus reborn—could defeat a plague of mutual distrust, even under the seething summer sky of a Vegas religious protest.

Chapter 5

RHYTHM OF GOD:
Mystery Tour

We were on our way to church as a family—Dad driving dutifully, Mom dressed nice, brother and me fidgety in our clip-on ties—with the car radio on, playing the current hit by the Beatles "Eight Days a Week." This was the mid-1960s, I was nine, and a great struggle was abroad in the land. Yes, a great venture was underway—the modern odyssey of the eternal soul—and we were in the thick of it, ready or not.

We were heading for church, but we were also moving headlong into new, unfamiliar territory. A modern economy of pop emotion and organized fun was gathering steam without any reference to religion, aiming to claim my blooming adolescent energies and intellect, challenging the world of settled faith.

The Beatles represented a vitality alien to the postwar workaday adult world. No one saw this music revolution coming, and no one could match it. It was a challenge to the congregational world, a threat to the church's emotional connection with us. Church would need to answer it, muster a response, meet the intensities of the new music with an intensity of its own, or lose a whole generation. Eight days a week, the culture was now cooking up its own confident commercialized brew, stirring young people to political self-consciousness and consumer power. The church has been playing catch-up ever since.

A couple of years later, the soul horizon was tested further when the Beatles' *Sgt. Pepper's* came out. The wallop came halfway through "Within You Without You" (cue minute 2:30). Enveloped in sonic textures of India, the song was a crashing meteor upon the surface of a suburban eleven-year-old's ordered routine. George Harrison was singing of human illusions and divine truth and the space between us all and the need for ultimate peace of mind lest you lose your own soul. It seemed a mix of Jesus and Vishnu and the soundboards of Abbey Road studio. The beat was polyrhythmic, the sound global. It declined the usual uplift and cheer of western pop. It dared to delay those pleasures in the name of some uncharted grown-up truth. As I heard it, there was no going back to former boyhood tranquility, no getting back, no wanting to go back. The big unscripted world of choice, risk, and experience had invaded.

I was a churchgoer, but I had a hunch the happy shiny kid-stuff emotion wouldn't save me. Something stronger must replace it or emerge from it. Life roared into the unknown: salvation a work in progress, never a sealed book. It sounded scary. But I sensed something providentially larger than ourselves was watching as we plotted the next move or blundered into it.

In other words, I was awakening to the existence of my own soul, which was powerfully radiating, registering the new conditions. I had to face its exacting presence.

It wasn't the Beatles' fault. They embodied energies coming from outside religious life that had been building for decades. Not coincidentally, the mainline church decline began around this time, and so did its ethical restraint on contemporary society. Congregations on the edges would soon grow—Pentecostal, nondenominational, megachurches. They would give the impression of becoming the new mainstream as media references to them multiplied. But in many cases their sectarian style and message were not designed to lead from the center. Christian influence in public life began to fade. The soul, more and more, was on its own.

The spiritual quest—the Jesus quest, too—did not end, of course. Neither did the quest of the soul, its demand to be acknowledged and honored if a human being is to mature and stay sane. The soul is a protest against the inhuman. In my time music became a unit of spiritual measure, a Rand McNally that charts the heat and motion of the soul, a way to greet it, walk with it.

It's a cliché that we're drenched in music now. After World War II, a revolution of rhythm entered the human body. Perhaps Elvis unleashed a secular Pentecost: rock 'n' roll took hold of the flesh and wouldn't let go. The next decades were a triumph of marketing and spiritual endeavor both. Today we all have our own soul music for meeting the day's tempestuous circumstance. Music declares a spirituality of the flesh that's far from the bookish spirit of classic theology. Dance pushes religion to repent of its suspicion of the body and to reconnect body and spirit.

I hung with church but needed music to fill in spaces that words weren't reaching. Music enhanced an argument that church had always made: an invisible life exists, and our well-being depends on staying attentive of it. Music was in a position to bridge the words of the gospel and the daily grit of secular routine.

That wasn't enough for me after a while. Life was piling up too high—the gale-force pressures of work, a divorce, my brother's mental illness, the death of a parent. For years I was listening to a lot of "sacred" music of the Renaissance. Now I was becoming suspicious of it. It sounded too pure, otherworldly, disconnected from real life. Sacred music—and the theme it pointed to, a vision of God-centered goodness and purity—seemed defeated by the world's interlocking problems and my own moody outlook.

This wilderness experience of fatalism kept its grip until one afternoon, when driving through snow, unhappy, unsure of the road ahead (literally and metaphorically), I heard the choral work of Estonian-born Arvo Pärt on the radio. It combined the sounds of Gregorian chant with intense modern harmonics. The result was a cleansing simplicity, gathering its stresses, then releasing them. It pulled me out of a stupor. Around the same time, friends put on a record one night by Canadian folk rocker Bruce Cockburn playing a song in which the narrator declares the urgent need to share the searchings and illuminations of his heart with someone else. That spirit must find human connection. "It only lives when you … give it away," he sings.[1] The surge of the groove defied the gravity of the day. I involuntarily zoned out of the dinner conversation to listen. I was hearing a confrontation with the emotional contradictions of life, my own included. The song was flagging the great humane paradox: find yourself by giving freely of yourself, and be saved. It stopped me in my usual tracks, sending me deep inside. Waiting there was the soul's underground life. With Cockburn as with Pärt, it felt like church. I heard truth borne on sound. Time to get back in the game. Out of the ruins, resolve. Out of brokenness, beauty.

This beauty is not some dainty flower of perfection. Pärt and Cockburn in very different ways catch a tough, leathery theological principle: emotional truth comes when I face the turmoil, not avoid it. Music lifts the veil on the contradictions that haunt every moment on earth—spirit versus flesh, dreams versus gravity, society versus solitude, aggression versus concord, love of God versus love of material security. Music makes it easier to face the truth that each of us carries a bundle of conundrums around wherever we go.

When music refuses to acknowledge this, it produces a white-bread playlist. But when it goes right, music summons something startling: the impulse to reconciliation, forgiveness of others, forgiveness of myself. It opens breathing space, a place for rest or defiance or regeneration.

Such breakthroughs can never be predicted. No musicologist can explain the power of the blues, Americana, or Arvo Pärt. Music reminds me that the soul is at work. It's traveling hard to reach the light.

Other sounds would soon come to my rescue. Jazz, folk, alternative, funk, roots, bluegrass, and reggae offered me a tougher armor to wear for facing the daily furies. They all give me something

> *But when it goes right, music summons something startling: the impulse to reconciliation, forgiveness of others, forgiveness of myself. It opens breathing space, a place for rest or defiance or regeneration.*

essential: spiritual realism. The music that matters makes way for God's nearness without whitewashing everyday heartbreak.[2]

"Music," critic George Steiner writes, ". . . has long been, it continues to be, the unwritten theology of those who lack or reject any formal creed."[3] Beautifully said. And yet. Music does point to religious truth. Hearing bluegrass (or Thelonious Monk or Emmylou Harris or Peter Gabriel) on Saturday night with friends feels to me like a warm-up to Sunday morning worship. Music moves the spirit in either of two directions, and I rely on it to take me both places, depending on the need of the moment—toward stillness and toward dance. Both directions—contemplation and action—are indispensable to the spiritual life, that is to say, to real life.

An ancient speculation says music escaped the taint of human sin at the beginning of the world. According to this idea, every song that melts the heart carries a sliver of original paradise, life before the Fall. The yearning that is embedded in gospel, symphony, bebop, or country stirs echoes of Eden. The familiar practice of chanting *Om* tries to recover an insight as old as creation—an endeavor to rediscover that original stillness, that first vibration. We have been trying to dream our way back to that ever since.

So when people say music is good for the soul, I take that to be a simple fact. It has saved me many times from pessimism. Music contains a message: you'll be okay. You'll make peace with time. The cosmos is your home after all.

The old hymns of childhood, their mood of tenderness and sobriety, make the same point: "A Mighty Fortress," "Be Still My Soul," "My Song Is Love Unknown," "What Wondrous Love Is This?" My affection for them grew in the slow drip of churchgoing through every season of personal family history. It's as if the hymns create a space, a room, a tiny stone chapel, for receiving the light. It's up to me to be there to do the receiving—show up, prepare the place, and be hospitable. One's soul is the dean of this modest chapel. But the soul can't be vigilant unless I am. I can't separate "me" from the soul, just as I can't detach "me" from my body. That seems to be the point. The soul guards, but it's a self-guarding, a self-knowledge.

In these ways music delivers a message straight from the unknown deep: don't underestimate me, the soul says. The musical pulse connects me to the soul's vital signs. It pulls me gently forward, as if to join a liturgical procession across the eons. Suddenly the turbulent past as I remember it loses force. It is released. It's no longer the inhibiting tyrant of my interior. It marches harmlessly past, blinking in the sun. A burden lifts. I can now confront the strong-pitched voices of the insistent present. The gates to the future swing open.[4]

The divine search gets distorted if I forget the soul's demands. Music wakes me up to this, this attempt at a planetary alignment: body, soul, and emotional focus. Together they create a frictionless moment of gratitude, and not even the heavy breathing of death can fog the windowpanes. At such a time, I feel revealed to the Creator.

The Beatles got all this started for me, this business of the soul's work, its obscure power, the high stakes. At the time it felt like life was handing me an unauthorized mix tape of exhilaration and danger. With the Fab Four, the Stones, James Brown, and the storm of

Sacred sonic encounters are possible every moment, if I keep the soul's chapel hospitable, and the doors open.

sound that followed, I felt a misalignment with church for years. I took it to be a conflict, but it was a false one. It would turn out to be a mystery tour. The music that matters is no echo of the chaos. Beethoven's late sonatas and Louis Armstrong and Stravinsky and Suzanne Vega and Howlin' Wolf and Jeff Coffin and David Olney and Steve Earle are never wrong-way detours. They are the way back and the way forward. Sacred sonic encounters are possible every moment, if I keep the soul's chapel hospitable, and the doors open.

Chapter 6

STORY OF GOD:
Rewriting the Darkness

I was driving home alone in the winter dark after the funeral, a 550-mile stretch of interstate after we buried my father. Staring into the frozen overcast night, I felt it staring right back.

So this was the real thing: this was a loneliness worse than all the songs about it. This was the life the adults don't mention when you're a kid. No music at hand on radio or device could break its grip. No jokes, friends, or poetry stood by. The world felt unsponsored, unwatched, unassured.

This wasn't the famous silence of God in a Swedish movie or some well-turned vignette to use in a short story. This was the dead-end silence oozing from this moment, stripped to its naked nasty facts. Even death was no great battle to face, just a ruthless commonplace that engulfs everybody, indifferent to bravery or prayer. I was taking it in at sixty-five miles per hour. This was the bedrock bleakness beneath the carnival of commerce. This was absence.

If this was the challenge of the dark and the password to a life without illusion, I didn't want to back down now, having come this far. Better to share the room with it, even a room as vast as the January night, and see what unfolds.

Official spirituality doesn't cover this. In the United States, we are talkative about God, assertive about what's out there, not what's not there. We even like to say we are especially favored by God, even when we have grave secret doubts about it.

I miss my father, a wry courtly southerner who died after a lot of illness and physical struggle. He was the family provider who said I should follow my own dreams and hunches, which meant following the writing. Where was he now? In a city graveyard. But where was he *really*? In heavenly peace? Watching me? Watching over me? A welcome thought, but it now seemed a little convenient and desperate.

Strange that the Bible says so little about the afterlife, about the status or mobility of souls after death—no detailed blueprint or floor plan on offer, just some sketchy evolving ideas that start with shadowy Sheol and end with bright heaven and fiery hell.

I drove on. Dad's absence presented itself now as a constant thought. His memory, my only link to him, has moved to the foreground since his death: a new presence. Absent, yet present. Is that just a clever paradox?

It was time to get gas and clear my head. The station was bustling, well-lit, like Hollywood make-believe, as if pretending that the howling realm of nonexistence wasn't just a breath away. The harsh light of the convenience store served as a handy image of the harshly aggressive world, where nothing is honored but the pursuit of power and survival. The pitiless interstate roar seemed to serenade

42

this theme—a deranged racetrack of competitors, a sweepstakes to see who can spend down the earth's oil first by driving their moaning metal machines the fastest. Life is equated with speed and violence, and victory goes to the clear-eyed warrior who takes what he wants without apology.

Others wandered into the store, browsing or business-like. All of us were perfect strangers, of course. Yet small mercies prevailed. We made eye contact. We commented on the weather ahead or behind, smiled, shared weary shakes of the head. Here were people acknowledging one another with flashes of kindness even on a raw night along the Darwinian blood-rimmed concourse known as I-40.

I bought popcorn and seltzer water and noticed the bumper stickers for sale:

The best vitamin for the Christian is B-1

I ♥ Jesus

Jesus loves the hell out of you

Under the circumstances, these merry sentiments looked a bit depleted and underprepared, outmatched by the colossal dark. I glanced out the store windows, at the big world, the empty night: *Jesus*. So easily the name comes. So easily we call out to it. It seems to cost nothing to say it, a taken-for-granted currency to spend and spend. It's a heavenly shield, a Sword of the Lord, a trinitarian talisman, as if the name alone provides protective cover.

But the word gets pulled, elongated, fatigued. Human demand tugs on it, stretches out the skin and casing of the word itself. You can hear it getting whirled and spun by the radio preachers: Jeeee-sus! It gets stuffed with every longing, every hope, despair, and lust. Nothing is checked at the door. We bring a welter of need and grief and desire: Jay-zus! It's a last stand, a flag to plant, a final bargaining chip, or I'm done for.

But it's a gnarly game, this imploring of the abstract word itself, *Jesus*. It easily gets cut off and biopsied from Jesus's own words, so that the mayhem of bigotry or warmongering or sex abuse gets done in his name. The bumper-sticker call-and-response disconnects it from the bigger turning wheel of life—from delight in the things God made, the outposts and bureaus of God's care, including this world itself.

I watched the other customers. We spoke or not. This was the South, in America, so no doubt most of the patrons that night carried in their heads snippets or notions about God whether they believed them or not—stories half-remembered about burning bush, parting sea, four thousand fed with a loaf of bread, walking on water, crucifixion, empty tomb, and a hundred other theological scraps and wonderments. Other people had taught them these things, or they overheard them. We were all the vessels of stories. We were all witnesses to what the night might be saying. We all had a choice of what to do with what we were hearing.

It was time to crank up the car and move on. I continued to host the nighttime absence. It was an unnerving guest, but I was getting used to it. I didn't even regret its arrival. It belonged in the fund of emotional facts that eventually arrive. It's a baseline. I didn't pray that it would disappear. Now, though, absence had to share space with these fresh images of people at the store, souls on a wing, lost or found. Absence, a messenger from the void, can't exist for long in (so to speak) a void. In the stirrings and yearnings of these strangers—all this created clay come to life and carrying crumbs of the story—something else comes calling too.

I got home safely, which felt like an accomplishment, a blessing. The darkness, though, still stiffly unmoved, conceded nothing, not one softening second of forgive-and-forget.

The long night wasn't over. The dog needed walking. Exhausted, blasted, I faced the outdoor big-top silence one more time. From its high perch the night looks confident, entitled, as if expecting to smother all challengers. But not tonight. Acts of human defiance are possible every moment. I walked along with my corgi sidekick and felt new affection for everything, every thing I could observe. I declared common cause with juniper bush, furtive red fox, and passing car: we were all in this together, all under the shadow of death on this planetary island of inexplicable life, the created world.

Everything I could touch—all was created, and all would die. But death was created too. This darkness was created. So these were all just details, predicates pointing to the main subject, a creator. The question was whether the tremors of Christmas and Good Friday and Easter reached far enough to touch them all, reached beyond neighborhood to ash heap, strip club, psychotic episode, and graveyard.

I was on the other side now, the far side of a night sojourn measured in miles and grief. My feet were planted again on heaving finite earth. The temptation to claim the barrenness of the night as a personal little Calvary passed quickly. It was a Genesis moment instead, a solidarity with everything else that must live, grow, move toward consciousness, face the abyss, and reckon with what's after. This is the connective tissue of creation—bolted down by gravity, sailing on language and music and DNA, assigned to wake up again to greet the morning after the furious night.

Two stories are at stake in this, depending on our choices. The nihilism story, full of shrieking dread and absence, is the first story, the original cosmic condition, and it would be the only one, the only narrative—if nothing in the universe had happened after it. But the second story, the God story, says the will of the divine wrote itself over the first story, the nihilistic one, and changed it. Genesis says God imposed creation upon the formless void and darkness. It doesn't say the write-over perfectly eclipsed or banished what was there. Void and darkness were not necessarily snuffed out or written out of the script in every detail. Those elements of the original chaos and nothingness still flash out from the backdrop. Shards and pieces still float free, crash into view, bruise the heart, attack cellular life, collide with people head-on.

The second story, the God story, must be regularly retold so that its bold lettering gets retraced upon the scroll of darkness. It's each person's choice to go with one of these stories, the God story or the nothingness story, and add a personal signature to it, deepening the grooves of the page. The world is not a cluttered scene of endless moving parts, but a narrative of simple lines trying to get written.

Something keeps renewing from within, a hidden photosynthesis. It's a matter of sunlight and oxygen touching some internal grid. Is that how God works?

Turning back toward the house on my midnight walk, I was getting clarity on the absence, one step at a time, the way it distorts life with its weapon of fear. The absence was just one more thing that happened in an evening: a unit of data. Even the absence is a mere created thing, something with a start and a finish. Even it moves downstream on the unstoppable river. The night's crowded details of creation finally push it off center, until next time.

Jesus walked this world, wandered this way. The memory clings to root and branch. The name *Jesus* doesn't magically contain all these things. The world is the container. It is touched and remembered by him. My loneliness lifted.

Why such thoughts on such a night? Something keeps renewing from within, a hidden photosynthesis. It's a matter of sunlight and oxygen touching some internal grid. Is that how God works? Merely asking the question, I experienced the photosynthesis again, out of the dark. A new thought arrived: the sovereignty of God means the divine force slips past the walls of despair and makes vigil with every intimate detail of teeming life. This is divine presence. A quantum of hope is unleashed.

All this talk of connectedness and internal blaze might read like a relentless mysticism, but it's literal, all of it: the heaviness of earth, the flow of time, the weight of grief, the daily dawn, the sudden turns of thought, all inescapably real. I reached the front door and took one look back across the neighborhood in the early-morning moodiness. Shining all along the street and hill were the usual porch lights of other houses—little lanterns in the cyclone of the unknown, little beacons signaling: we're alive. We're here. We're here if needed. We're here till further notice. We're here waiting, together.

Chapter 7

MOTION OF GOD:
Walk This Way

How strange the things that get remembered from first-grade Sunday school. What impressed me most was not learning the names of the twelve disciples or mastering the top ten hymns by Wesley. What gets me is all that walking they did in the Bible.

The treks of the patriarchs, the wanderings of the prophets, the momentum of the Jesus movement—walk speed was the mode of steady-spreading monotheism. For fifty years I've harbored a first-century fantasy: I should be walking to church and lots of other places, too.

When I was a kid going to church with the family, we drove past a dozen churches in order to get to ours in a neighborhood across town. I never understood this. We could have walked to two of them just down the block from the house. But no, we got fancy and drove. This was the postwar suburbs. America won World War II and prospered. We were entitled to spend money on new cars and cheap fuel. We drove.

Some time ago I returned home for a visit and planned to address this unfinished business: I'd walk to church. There was a congregation that meets a couple of blocks away, a trifling distance, but I was determined to test the theological potential of this oh-so-strange mode of transportation.

Inviting others in the family to go with me, I got just one taker, my brother. We set out. It was immediately satisfying. It felt good to travel light and decelerate. I could pay attention to street-level organisms—the massive oak trees, mockingbirds, bus stops, the smell of mowed grass, the Sunday paper waiting on the driveways. We walked past the headlines, keeping our destination up the street in view. Given enough walking time, I suppose we'd eventually reach the Holy Land where Jesus trod, even the primeval neighborhood where troubled ancestors Adam and Eve heard God walking fatefully toward them in the cool of the afternoon.

Instead, we walked a quarter mile to a place that stores all those Bible memories in its heart and mind, an A-frame church. We arrived a little sweaty but slid into a pew. The exercise increased the heart rate, enhancing our attention to the liturgy and especially the sermon, a fierce one from Luke 16, about the rich man and the hellish torments awaiting him for ignoring God's command of compassion.

Afterward it was good to walk back under the sun. It was good to walk off that sermon . . . or walk with it a while longer. The amble home kept the worship mood going, like a freelance recessional, expanding the church hour another twenty minutes. We enlisted all outdoor life in this postlude. It was a relief to subtract the vehicle from the Sunday morning equation for once—no need to find keys, crank up the engine, merge into traffic, and break the Sabbath spell.

These impressions add up. I will never forget my envy the first time I saw Orthodox Jews walking to the synagogue from all over their neighborhood. It was a scene of unplugged holiness, a life less distorted. I thought: that's how you do it. Arrange your priorities so the house of God is just blocks away.

A walk of any sort reestablishes a human-scale modesty about the cosmos, an off-the-grid perspective assumed by scripture but not by us. If circumstances allow, even a short stretch of walking—a twenty-minute break—is enough to reclaim the body, remember dreams, assess one's mood, declutter one's space. New ideas or solutions shoot up from an unspoken artesian mental well. Walking seems to release some sort of secret. I can't shake the thought that it might save my life.

Part of what's interesting about walking, what keeps me on the trail of it, is the quaint modern resistance to it. The times seem offended by the very idea of a stroll. From the perch of the economic fast track, walking implies you can't afford a car (true, many people can't), or, worse, you're in no hurry. Walking, you're taking a break from globalization. You're doing something besides pursuing money or spending it. You're out of reach of marketers. Walking is the transportation industry equivalent of writing longhand—a way to slow down your thoughts. Walking, you are doing what others privately suspect they ought to be doing.

"If by fate or by Providence you happen to find yourself in a wandering way, try not to listen to the voices in your head telling you that wandering is wrong or wasteful," historian Stephen Prothero writes. "Nothing is going to die, and something might actually be born, if you turn off your computer, leave your 'real work' behind, and go out on a wander without any particular purpose or destination in mind."[1]

Walking is no stunt. It's a small act of rebellion. Walking rewrites the definitions of acceptable speed and progress. It can be an eyes-wide-open prayer. Like prayer, a walk is a shoving aside of the in-your-face demands rushing toward you.

Interesting details release and shimmer. You notice teenagers roaring past in cars they pretend to control, and it triggers memories of one's own adolescent days of mach-speed immortality. Then the street traffic disappears again, and the silence feels strange—no kids outside playing pick-up football in the era of video games and podcasts.

Walking, be prepared to confront your own ignorance. I regularly walk with the dog to a peaceful hilly patch of land. It happens to be a cemetery. Every time I wander among the crumbling gravestones, some of them two hundred years old, I am seized by the old habit of stepping respectfully over the graves, never on them, as a show of respect. Do the dead care about this courtesy? Are they otherwise occupied? Is a cemetery just the way station on the path to afterlife glory, or is it the ultimate delete file? I feel like I've walked in on a theology seminar in my head, and I'm not prepared. But a walk in such precincts at least puts me closer to the action, the undeniable facts of the grave.

Walking, a person gets reacquainted with the surface of the planet. On a stroll, the ground rules of creation are

> *Walking is no stunt. It's a small act of rebellion. Walking rewrites the definitions of acceptable speed and progress. It can be an eyes-wide-open prayer.*

reasserted. I notice the way the earth patiently endures us, suffers us, absorbing our violent fevers and projects, our pollution and grindings and leavings. A walk offers a momentary truce. It gives me a fighting chance to see the planet anew and even try to recover a just relationship to it. Writer Martin Amis talks about the urgency of seeing the pummeled earth with as fresh or innocent an eye as possible. "As the planet gets progressively less innocent, you need a more innocent eye to see it," he says.[2]

In some such way, a walk might be regarded as a penance, a godsend. Henry David Thoreau thought of it as a sanctified adventure. He was a fearsome walker (four hours a day) who preferred to saunter, a word that possibly stems from "sainte terre," or holy land. So a saunterer is a holy-lander, he said. Every walk is a kind of pilgrimage.

"So we saunter toward the Holy Land, till one day the sun shall shine more brightly than ever he has done, shall perchance shine into our minds and hearts, and light up our whole lives with a great awakening light, as warm and serene and golden as on a bankside in autumn," he wrote.[3]

I take it that the gospel was first heard and spread at a saunter, in a world-bending spirit of enterprise, flinging wide its net. Jesus's "Follow me" implied a democratic impulse. People walked with him, behind him, or away from him (and he healed many who couldn't do it on their own).

With such thoughts in mind, one recent Saturday morning I went on a neighborhood prayer walk, sponsored by my church. The purpose was to walk a few downtown blocks for an hour, pray discreetly for our town, and stretch our own spiritual muscles with this unusual task.

The minister asked us to go in groups of two or three, greet people on the street, and take along a small bottle of water that she had blessed, water to sprinkle here and there as a sign of divine grace.

She urged us to keep a spirit of curiosity on our sojourn. I was a little apprehensive at first. How will this play out? I wasn't interested in muscling in on someone else's weekend morning. And I wasn't accustomed to toting holy water around, even if the container was the modest size of a shampoo sampler. Enough: I decided to stop my internal babble. The idea of this walk sounded good-hearted and unassuming, not a florid engagement of spiritual warfare. Onward.

I was surprised to notice so many houses and small businesses I never noticed before, some new, some bustling, some in disrepair: these were my neighbors. So much we have in common even though I've never met them. We share a town, a commitment to public prosperity and order and the education of the young. We share the same dramas of weather, the annual local parades, the tax rates, the collective memories.

We're preoccupied with the same stubborn mighty questions. Does God exist? Does God pay attention to us? How do we connect? How do we satisfy this restlessness? How do we face doubts and regrets?

Big questions, and I discover it's not a bad idea to field them at a slow stroll. An intuition rises unshakably: these unanswered questions contain pregnant revelations within themselves, if I take the time to walk with them. Walking is a kind of waiting in motion, a waiting alongside the day's details for the fullness of time.

You might say that not much happened on the prayer walk that day. My small posse said good morning to some joggers, swung past the craft fair and perused the wares, said a little prayer for the traffic barreling by, noticed some newly boarded-up shops, enjoyed the warm weather, and circumspectly sprinkled the holy water along the way.

Something else was accomplished—a new vantage point on an ordinary Saturday. On a walk you can see unspoken connections between us all. You sense some invisible lines that join us. As a small group, we got to know one another a little better. We learned of others in the congregation or the town who needed help, who needed people. Staying in touch: there's no other solution. The edifice of life is fragile, uncertain. We should approach one another with respect and mutual support.

"When we rise from sleep let us rise for the joy of the true Work that we will be about this day, and considerably cheer one another on," writes John McQuiston II in a little book I keep close by, *Always We Begin Again: The Benedictine Way of Living*. "Each day carries the potential to bring the experience of heaven; have the courage to expect good from it. Be gentle with this life, and use the light of life to live fully in your time."[4]

It seems to me a lot happened out there that morning. A walk unpacks all sorts of news, enacting a ritual purification, a simplification, a reconnect, a way to cheer each other on. A fog of isolation and alienation—nettlesome distortions of God and one another—was lifted for a time. I could have walked on and on, enjoying a rare contentment, a need of nothing else, a feeling of balance between earth and sky, between questions and answers. That morning a small unlikely group of people, daring to take a walk, dared to bless. And be blessed.

Chapter 8

MIRACLE OF GOD:
True and False

O nce during a big arena revival, I saw a man on stage with a shortened arm straighten it out so it returned to normal length, while the evangelist shouted praise to Jehovah God. The audience cheered at this healing miracle. The man and his now-celebrated arm were hustled off to the backstage darkness before I could get a closer look.

On another stage, another night, an older man was escorted to the podium, where the preacher healed his deafness. I followed him back to his seat and tried to interview him. He couldn't hear me.

I've seen a weeping icon at a church (it was on a tour, traveling from town to town). Hundreds of people crowded around it. It seemed to glisten, but I have to confess I didn't see tears.

I've seen the image of Jesus on a screen door. People came far and wide to witness it. It was a nighttime phenomenon that depended on the next-door neighbors keeping their porch light on so the image could appear just right. It always looked like Willie Nelson to me.

I once interviewed a woman who told me that her friend cured himself of AIDS by sheer willpower and meditation. I asked for proof, medical records, any kind of documentation, and never heard from her again.

The subject of miracles is a wild ride and, for a writer about religion, a professional dilemma. I've seen plenty of stage miracles. I can't say I was moved by any of them. Either they looked faked or they glorified the performer. Even the impressive ones left questions. What is the point of this? Should faith depend on these miracles? Should they be a test of belief? Do they express the presence of God? Do they distort the intentions of God? Perhaps they were signs of grace that were denied to me. Or maybe they were lost on me because I wasn't looking for them to happen. Perhaps, as poet Joseph Brodsky wrote, miracles "know just where people will be waiting."[1]

Strange and wondrous things exist. Unexplained healings happen. So do everyday frauds and delusions. Reporting on these matters large and small, I found it impossible to please anyone. Believers accused me of a hardened heart, an agenda to destroy the church. Skeptics assailed me as an idiotic dupe for giving so-called miracles any coverage at all.

How peculiar it is, the miracle business. Its main effect seems to be to leave people exasperated, bamboozled, or divided. It becomes a dubious tournament among believers, a game of chicken: anyone in the congregation who dares to doubt the miracle in their midst runs the risk of being a traitor, never quite trustworthy again.

Defenders explain miracles as visible signs that God plants among us to keep our spirits up. Yet they never overpower or cancel out the world's anti-miracles, the daily outbreaks of murderous gunfire, rapes, and carnage of war. It's hard to see how the savage human world is slowed down or reversed by media-fascinated miracles.

Despite these caveats, I've often prayed for a miracle myself— the healing of my brother's mental illness. He lives still with my mother, wholly dependent on her, unable to work or drive. There's been no change in his condition in forty years. Still I pray. I pray that God will bless him and be present with him. And I believe these prayers are answered.

For years now, for instance, he has been the most consistent churchgoer I know. Regular worship requires no prompting, no fuss. He dresses up and quietly goes, walking the two blocks every Sunday morning. It's one of the few things he does reliably and independently.

His illness requires planning—making sure his meds are re-filled and paid for, finding structure for his day, deciding where he will eventually live. His situation is an education in patience. It has forced me to learn something about the intricacies of the human mind and human suffering and about what love requires despite these obstacles. My brother has been my teacher through all this, and my prayer ultimately is gratitude for his life no matter what, and for my mother for these decades of care, and for my wife for agree-ing to help take on these responsibilities.

Sometimes a questioning little voice pipes up: Are you praying hard enough? Shouldn't you put more toil into praying for a mirac-ulous healing? But there's something questionable about the ques-tions, as if the key to the whole thing depends on the quality of my prayers, my coaxing and sweet-talking of the Lord—my will, not God's. All I can say to that is, well, look around: the whole world needs healing and praying over. There's no end to the amount of prayer needed on all fronts.

Yes, the miraculous is a hazardous subject. It's hard to find the right distance on it, the right gaze. There's a tendency to focus too hard on it, or not enough; to spend too much time on it, or not enough.

I have to take my cues and clues from the Gospel record. What's found there is surprising. Jesus isn't on the scene very long before he starts healing people. Yet it was no easier then than it is now to get an accurate read on what was happening. Many rejected what they saw him do, or they said it was the devil's work. The reader finds Jesus warning people, time after time, to stay quiet about the healings.

He must have had his reasons. So much could go wrong in the retelling: the healed person's report could be distorted, misremembered, shot with exaggerations. It would escalate the anger against this Galilean healer. It would overshadow Jesus's long-term message of the reign of God. In the Gospel of Mark, things were happening fast. Jesus hadn't had time yet even to pick a solid group of disciples or do some basic preaching, then lepers got in his face. He had the power to do something about it, so he did.[2]

So I count myself as a skeptic within the believing world—a believer in the Christian creeds but a skeptic about phenomena that derail bigger issues.

Many a denomination, adopting Jesus's apparent caution about miracles, is reluctant to endorse them without deliberation and care. Disputable things in gospel life ought to be secondary to the messages that unite.

So I count myself as a skeptic within the believing world—a believer in the Christian creeds but a skeptic about phenomena that derail bigger issues. A miracles skeptic should be open to testimony, open to their possibility, but not be hemmed in by one cherished interpretation of events, one tyrannical reading of scripture or life that bullies people into one deep-dish doctrinal stance.

Behind such coercion runs specific theories about how God works, as if we know. One theory says: there have been no more miracles since the close of the Apostolic age. Another declares: new scripture is being written today, with miraculous signs that herald the end of time. Theories have a certain beauty, and it's tempting to let the beauty outshine and outrank any new facts that could upset, upend, or nullify it. Too much theorizing distorts the flow and fluidity of the present moment, including the next reading of the ancient text, the next intuitive turn and reception.

Hasty affirmations of the latest miracle discount a particular divine gift, human reason. People have an ethical duty to size up facts about the way the world really works. Without that, reports of specious miracles multiply. Suddenly they are everywhere. Coincidences become signs of spiritual warfare. Other people get demonized in a tidal wave of paranoia. Then the blood really flows.

No: on the Christian horizon there's only one miracle that counts, with evidence from history that the usual storm of contemporary miracles doesn't possess. It took place long ago, and the existence of the church cannot be explained without it: the Resurrection. On Good Friday afternoon, the disciples were defeated, scattered, ashamed at the grisly death of their leader. By Easter morning, they had experienced a shocking reversal of heart and mind. Their dead leader was alive, they said, and now they eagerly risked their lives to tell the news in the very teeth of a hostile empire. And they were martyred for it, though not before they did the unforeseeable, the inconceivable: they created a fast-spreading collection of communities that similarly experienced the risen Lord. Something has to account for that reversal of circumstance in human history. If the Resurrection is at the very center of Christian belief and behavior, then I don't see any urgent reason to vote up or down on other miracles since in Jesus's name.

Of course, old questions swoop in and try to take over, in grim tones of interrogation. Did Jesus *physically* rise from the dead? Was the Easter event just a *metaphor* for the spiritual reawakening of the disciples? What would videotape have shown on Easter morning? Where are the bones of Jesus? Interesting questions, but a bigger one lurks: was the Resurrection a historical event, or not? A major piece of evidence has to be faced—the existence of the church, some four million of them worldwide now. Why are they here at all? How do we account for them? The burden of explanation falls as heavily on secular historians and nonbelievers as on church apologists.

The historical persistence of the church gets loosely dismissed as a mass hallucination. Doubters declare that a miracle is something that by definition can't happen. Okay then: if the Resurrection happened, then we'll have to call it something other than a miracle.

My own search for an undistorted faith doesn't depend on theological hysterics, paranormal theories, precise doctrinal wording, or lightning strikes of privileged personal revelation. It embraces the dizzying idea that the Resurrection outlasts all the debates about it.

Whatever else it was, it was a historical event. Believers reacted to the risen appearances of Jesus in real time. They experienced the presence of God as an incarnation in time and place. Philosopher and skeptic William Gass once quipped: "A miracle is something that cannot happen, and shouldn't, and won't again, but has occurred all the same, despite laws, odds, expectations."[3] Something deeply strange happened long ago, in history, on earth, and it takes both faith and reason to make sense of it.

My own search for an undistorted faith doesn't depend on theological hysterics, paranormal theories, precise doctrinal wording, or lightning strikes of privileged personal revelation. It embraces the dizzying idea that the Resurrection outlasts all the debates about it. Providential motion casts its shadow over our days, and it's within the reach of anyone by the powers of reason, a spirit of inquiry, and the persistence of grace.

To me this places each of us in the position of one of novelist Walker Percy's existential castaways—washed up on the shore, no real clue about where we are, but free to poke around and collect evidence and try to get to the bottom of things, get the hang of the place. We are free to notice people, aid their troubles and pains, join their dreams of wholeness, their lunge toward serenity—why are they made that way? We notice houses of worship, those preserves of ancient testimony and arguments—why do they endure? Evidence of an inexplicable world is at hand—the miracle of language, sunshine, wildflowers, jazz, jokes, the speed of light. The canvas of action is a big one. The ministrations of God reach across time, just in time.

Chapter 9

HOUSE OF GOD:
Situation Room

Once during the exchange of the peace at church, I turned routinely to the pew behind me to shake hands with whoever was there.

"Peace be with you," I said to a guy, barely making eye contact.

"Do you have five dollars," he said.

He looked homeless and in a hurry. He was alone. He now held my gaze.

"I'll pay you back next week," he added.

I don't know which was more remarkable: the church-hour request or the precision of the amount requested or the pledge to pay it back. I was not sure how to proceed. I was too dismayed to think.

I could have ignored him or smiled and said sorry no or moved aside with him to discuss it further or taken him to lunch. Or called the police.

But I had the money and gave him a $5 bill, not in a spirit of saintly compassion but frank annoyance. People were staring. I turned back around to face the worship ritual, which was murmuring steadily onward and had not stopped for any unusual financial transactions underway in the fifth row.

It broke all the rules, this little cash advance. He asked for money during worship! A shakedown during the exchange of the peace! Exploitation and extortion!

Could I have handled it differently? Did I cave in to sentimental guilt by giving him money at all? Or should I have handed him the $20 bill also that peeked out of my wallet?

As the moment passed, I thought I had failed a test. I felt mocked by the Gospel line: "For where two or three are gathered in my name, I'm there with them" (Matthew 18:20). Mr. Homeless and I were, momentarily, two. That made it official, according to Gospel arithmetic: Jesus made it a triad. There we were, eye to eye in the house of God, bringing with us our own particular versions of poverty.

I don't know what the exchange was like for him, but to me it demonstrated the upside-down world that is church, a place that engages me but more often exposes me.

Much of the time it's nearly impossible to look at church and see it aright, see it for what it is: a chamber where the normal laws of gravity are suspended. It's a crucible where sacred and profane jostle and try to make peace. It's a ragtag encampment of wanderers throwing their future in with a juggernaut of the divine. Take away the parking lot and the video screen and microphone, and the place is no different from a dusty Christian catacomb of year 150 CE: a beleaguered, shuffling miracle.

No ancient historian could have bet on the survival of the church, its expansion across the reckless centuries, or the endurance of the news that churches report: the presence of the biblical God at the center of the human drama. No anthropology satisfactorily explains these strange facts: the arrival of monotheism in history, the survival of the Jews, the life and death and resurrection of the Nazarene named Jesus, the power of the gospel as recently as this morning to change a person's life or millions of others.

From such an angle, a church building no matter how humble is the indigestible oddball of the secular age. By any scientific account it shouldn't be there at all. Yet there it is.

The strangeness of this is hard to see amid the familiar roar that surrounds modern religion, whether it's the protests of the doubters or the certitudes of the moralists. It's said that church is a hospital for sinners, a safe harbor in an uncertain world, or quite the contrary, a place of repugnant superstition. We do know church is a place of satire-worthy routine. Some families sit in the same pew week after solemn week for generations. Or the sermon always starts at nineteen minutes after the hour (and is nineteen minutes long—or nineteen minutes too long). This faction doesn't speak to that faction. And, yes, yes, the place is full of hypocrites. Or it's water-logged with boredom. All these things are true, and they are all the least interesting thing about a church, any church.

The day I was accosted by the $5 supplicant—a short worship service on a weekday—was a day I had snuck over

No ancient historian could have bet on the survival of the church, its expansion across the reckless centuries, or the endurance of the news that churches report: the presence of the biblical God at the center of the human drama.

from the newsroom where I worked, just a block away. It had been a typical morning on the job. I was on the phone getting a story about a popular local minister who was on the verge of being fired. (Why? Financial abuse? Sexual misconduct? No one was talking, yet.) A twitchy local guy had left a nine-hundred-page manuscript for me in the lobby that detailed the end of the world as told to him personally by the Lord. (He wanted it printed in tomorrow's paper word for word.) Meanwhile, the editors wanted summaries of two other stories from me for the weekend editions right now—two articles as yet unwritten. My head was pounding. I got over to church.

If a church service can be described as a citadel of serenity against the storms of this life, well, it seldom starts out that way. I can always hear the dominion of the devouring world outside—the yammering honks of traffic, the pedestrian snarls. They seem jealously determined to spoil the quiet. I bring my own internal uproars to the sanctuary, too, a howling bundle of grievance and need. No use pretending otherwise. But then, at such a service, the minister will make a fortunate decision. She'll have us sing. One time it might be Julie Miller's "All My Tears" or the folk song "I Wonder As I Wander."

We'd sing them slowly and sweetly with great good help sometimes from an ensemble of bluegrass instrumentalists. With the final notes wafting skyward, the room was stilled. There we sat, ready and waiting, resistance seeping away. The parcel of questions everybody carries along through life—Is God here? Is there a message here for me, for us? What do I do next?—was readying for a reckoning.

Out of the noonday turmoil came a moment of beauty. Somehow, we had all found our way here, and now something was gathering in the sanctuary's visuals, aromas, and acoustics: something like goodness was released. It wasn't liberal compassion or conservative decency or a crowd-sourced spirit of community. It was something older, something launched long ago, a ship on the open water, breaking the horizon, moving each moment closer, heading toward us, through us, pulling us forward into future time. What unfolds at church, whether my receptors are functioning that day or not, is the culmination of everything that was set in motion all those centuries ago and now blossoms in present time.

Churches disagree on a thousand points of theology or worship or politics. But they share something more important than any difference, an unspoken charter with a precise message: you have a soul, and this is its guesthouse. Come on in. If you want it, you can sign up for good works down the hall. If you want it, silence awaits through those double doors over there: the sanctuary. Don't be afraid.

Stroll the halls and something might rise from the depths: your life talking to you. The metrics of Sunday are different from those of the rest of the week. The church's transmissions generate signals that you won't hear elsewhere: the adventure of life under God is more reliable, more interesting than the promises of stock market or Internet Cloud. If you want it, you can sign on for the upending of the world's priorities.

All this might sound excessively otherworldly, but if it's true, then it is as practical as it is mystical. It embodies a wised-up counterculturalism that a person needs for surviving the swindles and self-deceptions of modern life. Congregations are the last places in America, the very last, where time is set aside for values and motives that don't promote relentless ideologies or monetized product placement or the law of raw self-interest or the digital Fear of Missing Out. Church says: we will honor things that might well embarrass everyday society—reverence, prayer, vulnerable emotion, the arc of invisible mysteries, eruptions of gratuitous giving, the setting aside of the celebrated ego, and the pledging of thankless acts of mercy that defy materialistic advantage. If these things are an embarrassment, bring it on.

Embedded in the sinews of a church is an unlikely skepticism—a wariness of the world's gregarious boasts and flaws. As the faith teaches, be alert to the old-fashioned seven deadly sins—pride, greed, envy, gluttony, lust, wrath, and sloth—before buying into the latest tidal wave of wishful thinking, magical thinking, positive thinking. Gospel values of sacrifice, fair play, and rejoicing are there to push back against self-pity, cruelty, utopian politics, and personal chaos.

Jesus set the example. He tripped up respectable thinking. He questioned public power, even public prayer. He refused to flatter the rich and powerful and threw curveballs to everyone else. The first shall be last. The meek shall inherit. The reign of God is near, very near. Abundant life isn't precisely the same thing as a four-car garage. Death isn't the last word. A Galilean carpenter, not a comic-book superhero, becomes the world's savior.

Worship therefore is a regularly scheduled provocation, a weekly situation room in which people come to sort out the story and get it straight. It's where believers get their metaphors and marching orders for carrying on another week just in case he doesn't return this time around. Each person renews the seeds of her own transformation. So does each church.

These large claims for church might sound preposterously alien to the congregation you know. The disconnect is a big part of the miracle: churches exist despite their own ineptitude and difficult personalities. Somehow they were built by people who managed to put aside personal vexations and a perpetual lack of funds and who instead focused on divine hunches and heroic trust, including trust in one another.

No church gets everything right, naturally. A church down the street exalts the Great Commission rather than the Sermon on the Mount. Another is more comfortable with Calvary than Resurrection. The one across the road goes with spiritual diversity, not the details of the Trinity. Elsewhere, the preacher quotes Paul of Tarsus more than Jesus of Nazareth. These differences depend on congregational temperament, local sociology, or the minister's specific seminary training and favorite reading list.

Ever since Jesus, the world has been thrown off balance. So have the churches. He left no instruction manual for organizing denominations or enforcing clergy credentials. He didn't diagram the fine print of doctrine. He didn't discourse on tragedy. He didn't explain terminal illness and earthquakes. But the news of his resurrection kept people together. When enormity is too great for words, churches keep a light burning. There comes a time to shut up and take action—write a check, give blood, unload a truck,

> *Ever since Jesus, the world has been thrown off balance. So have the churches. He left no instruction manual for organizing denominations or enforcing clergy credentials. He didn't diagram the fine print of doctrine. He didn't discourse on tragedy. He didn't explain terminal illness and earthquakes.*

71

take in a refugee, or pray prayers of biblical proportion. None of this requires doctrinal hairsplitting or ecclesiastical convention, but all of these are made possible by a church's open doors.

I was feeling flattened out after a long week when the guy behind me asked for money that day at church. The encounter, my end of it, could have gone better, been infused with more depth and high spirits. We might have gone out for coffee, become friends. It all happened fast. No, he didn't come back the next week. I never saw him again. Not yet, anyway. I'll turn around again in the pew next time and see what there is to see in this place of surprises. Jesus keeps coming in at odd angles. It requires a turn in his direction.

Chapter 10

TIMETABLE OF GOD:
Ministry of Fear

I first met awe by staring at the sky. The curving ocean of blue-ceiling silence was the overwhelming baseline of childhood. That's surely the feeling of most children. But in the South, the sky was always something more. It was the staging area for disaster that might arrive any of three ways: by tornadoes, Russian missiles, or Jesus Christ returning in calamitous glory. We gazed up at it with amazement and alarm.

We learned of tornadoes from *The Wizard of Oz*, the USSR nuclear arsenal from Walter Cronkite, and the Second Coming from the tracts left on the windshield. One way or another, the sky was a messenger of doom, a potential furnace that could wipe out our future in an instant. We had an unobstructed view of it from my Louisiana elementary school yard—our lookout post for funnel clouds, Sputnik mischief, and biblical prophecy.

As it turned out, tornados were mercifully rare, and the Russians were no-shows. The Second Coming, however, stayed on the docket. The connoisseurs of Protestant apocalypse made sure of that. For as long as I can remember, I've been cornered, buttonholed, and prayed over by these frowning tribunes of Bible interpretation. Their tireless crusade was a hazard of a Cold War childhood—later, I discovered, an occupational hazard in a career of writing about religion in America in any era. I learned much from them.

These grim reapers gravitated toward me. I was a shy kid who was happy to get along. I didn't keep a forceful counterargument in my back pocket. I had been issued no talking points at my Methodist church. What we said at worship was, "Christ has died, Christ is risen, Christ will come again"—no detailed itinerary on that last part. It wouldn't occur to our minister to devote a month's worth of sermons to the theme of doomsday. There were other things to preach about Jesus. The end of the world would take care of itself. The Methodists, like other large mainline denominations, ran a vast network of ministries, schools, agencies, and publishing houses. They believed goodness could unfold in day-to-day life on earth if we work at it, with Jesus at our side. The Armageddon guys on radio and TV, by thunderous contrast, were freelancers, anti-institutionalists. They disdained the denominations' cautious scriptural readings, the churches' fiscal responsibilities, their centuries of gospel witness.

I didn't grasp this at the time. The end-timers looked like confident grown-ups with a frightening message and an unbeatable brand. I thought it was the charitable Christian thing to hear them out. They, for their part, strongly advised that I repent and prepare to get raptured to heaven or be left behind in the gory tribulation under the dictatorship of the fabled Antichrist. "Turn or burn," declared the church marquee signs. Accept the Four Spiritual Laws, chirped my little school friends clutching their pamphlets. "You may never have this opportunity again," intoned Billy Graham on the TV.

This was not the Jesus of the stained-glass windows at church, where he gently gathered sheep and beckoned children. I thought of him as the walking, companionable presence of God, the Son of Man dispensing parables, the Good Shepherd offering words of redemption. The mainliners were trying to be true to a larger picture of Jesus that isn't swallowed up by the writhing rhetoric of apocalyptic interpretation. And they were resented for it.

The doomsayers had a better sense of publicity and mass behavior than we did. To them, the very headlines of our time were maneuvering the cosmic endgame into place—all those late twentieth-century rumors of European union and one-world government stoking a bonfire of apprehension. They didn't refer much to the Galilean. Perhaps they were bored with the Jesus who had lived and taught and turned the world upside down. They tiptoed around him.

Their evasiveness is understandable: Jesus had warned against obsessing about the end-timing, the hour and the day. In Mark he says: "Heaven and earth will pass away, but my words will certainly not pass away. But nobody knows when that day or hour will come, not the angels in heaven and not the Son. Only the Father knows."[1] The armageddonists had other ideas. To them, the Messiah's main action hadn't taken place yet. Perhaps Jesus was an awkward failure the first time around. Maybe the First Coming never got traction, since the world's still a rotten place.

In the 1970s, the book *Late Great Planet Earth* sold more than ten million copies. As a teenager, I despised its garish descriptions of doom—and yet fell briefly under their sway. I mournfully chose high school graduation, a normally festive rite, to give a copy to a classmate, for his own good. I'd like to apologize to him now.

As it turns out, the only impressive thing about the end-time stuff, century after century, is its 100-percent failure rate. Yet the discredited prognosticators keep coming back. They understand the power of fear to worm its way into our psyches and obliterate trust in a 3,500-year-old biblical message that says God made creation and said it was good.

But there comes a time to walk away from retail mental slavery. These pessimistic impulses have more to do with the turbulences of U.S. history and sociology than with religion.[2] They have more to do with the psychology of the nuclear threat and the fear about a changing society than with gospel truth. "Fear not," it says in the Bible more than forty times. It's as if scripture has to keep hitting the reset button and wipe the fright out of people so they can think straight and hear its messages without distortion and panic.

Standing above and behind this is the greatest question of all: "One way or another, does God preside over all this—*care about all this*—or not?" The Genesis story of creation, in outline and sinews, gives answer: God went to the trouble to make the world, and God sustains it each instant, and God will bring it to a new beginning according to God's own timetable. To disparage or disrupt or revise that story is to assert God is failing against the forces of chaos and devilment. The ancient Egyptians had a cosmology that depended on the air-god Shu standing tall on the earth and holding up the weight of heaven so it wouldn't crush everything below.[3] The logic of biblical monotheism strips away such florid imagery. There's one creation, sponsored by one Creator, overarching, beyond all efforts to decode or domesticate. It is dependent on no human explanation or mythology.

It's still a riddle to me that so much of religion's time, including my own, can be taken up by overheated end-of-days soap operas. But probably there will always be a fan base for apocalyptic anxiety. One-fifth of polled Americans believe they'll live to see ultimate Armageddon. No one talks about the real anxiety that often drives this impulse: the simple wish to avoid death. Add to that the hubris of each generation to believe that it has been chosen to witness the end. Add another unmentionable: the itch to evade responsibility for the mess we have made of politics, family life, earth care, and the command of love of neighbor. End-of-days obsessions practically announce: "We're done with God's earth. We give up on ourselves and one another. Let's move on to the next thing, *now*." Let's take the script away from God and do a rewrite.

What civilization needs is a crash course not in the Mark of the Beast but in the marks of an incarnational theology, a tour of the world where the elements of creation are sacramental signs, God's fingerprints on earth, wind, fire, and present time, the ingredients of a faith unencumbered by the era's unique distractions. Incarnation means eternity has been bent to touch the poor comings and goings of planet Earth in its orbit. Incarnation stands

> *What civilization needs is a crash course not in the Mark of the Beast but in the marks of an incarnational theology, a tour of the world where the elements of creation are sacramental signs, God's fingerprints on earth, wind, fire, and present time.*

lodged in the sizzling atoms, in the oratorios of Handel, in barnyard filth, in eye contact, all a poetry in motion.

Can this moment be an adequate vessel of fulfillment and joy, or not? "We are living in a world that is absolutely transparent, and God is shining through it all the time," writer-monk Thomas Merton once declared.[4] Our capacity for wonder was made for this.

The first sacramental fact is the sky: by day, the lines of horizon and stratosphere look like God's abstract painting still drying, the canvas still getting touched up. By night, the cascade of stars adds a fearsome dimension—the unspeakable empty distances of outer space. A measure of it is restored to humanity by the power of a story of Magi following a star to a little hut in an earthen beige desert town at Christmastime.

The sky is a constant reminder of terrible divine power: glorious weather can turn deadly within the hour. This is humbling. It's difficult to abide. So we go indoors and spin out our own stories. At least by stepping outside a person can enjoy the sun-beamed sky and notice other vistas. Under this same sky Jesus felt the breeze and said the wind goes where it will and so does the Spirit. Every sunrise is a sign of renewal of this world's continued existence, another daily chance to get things right under Someone's watch.

It took a while before I could look at the sky again and see it not as a tarmac of dread but as the canvas of origins, an unfinished cosmos. I eventually realized that such a sky is big enough to absorb the latest doomsday delirium without a blink. It is a window on infinity, caught and framed by time.

"Blessed is the day when the youth discovers that within and above are synonyms," said Ralph Waldo Emerson.[5] When I look at the sky now, I don't feel consternation. I don't look for a sign in the sky. The sky *is* a sign. It's the largest piece of evidence of divine endeavor that we have. It's what we have until we see God.

> The sky is what's there until we see God—
> the roof of everything, impossible to trace.
> An argumentative itch says it doesn't exist,
> the sky: it's just a fancy scattering of sun rays,
> a blues figment, the smear of atmosphere.
> Talk all you want: sky obliges us
> with shelter for the circus act of argument.
> Sky-watching and silent prayer
> come to this: They send foolish words away,
> eventually all words.
> I thank God the sky is no symbol:
> it bears down, ablaze, inconceivable—
> what's there until we see God.

Chapter 11

IMAGE OF GOD:
Entourage

Imagine this, if you dare: whenever a human being walks past you, a posse of angels is right there hard at work, silently yet forcefully announcing, "Behold, the image of God!"[1]

If this old and extravagant rabbinical teaching is true, then it's time I reassess my experience of, say, New York's Grand Central Terminal. The bustling tableau of America's great train station now becomes imbued with a shocking sanctity, a teeming interior brightness almost too much to bear. This goes for *any* human exchange no matter how rushed or routine.

I first heard this lushly angelic idea—flanks of angels deployed to keep custody of the image of God and its human vessel—in a small crowded room at a book festival in Nashville. A few minutes before, I had spoken about a book I'd written on Ecclesiastes. After me came writer Marjorie Thompson, who was there to talk about spiritual practice. And she began by describing this image of angels, which was first espoused by Joshua ben Levi of the third century CE.

People gasped at hearing it. One of the gasps was mine. A few people started weeping. What was happening?

Minutes before, when I was speaking, those gathered in the room were Protestants, Catholics, Jews, Muslims, Hindus, Buddhists, seekers, or skeptics. When they heard the angel story from Marjorie, all dividing lines melted away. The meaning of truth shifted to something more primal than denominational creed. We were given permission to imagine, or remember, that the image of God is part of our resume and destiny. Maybe it was a secret theological hunch all along, never admitted. Now it was out in the open, and in that moment it blessed everyone there.

The image of God is a revolutionary idea with ramifications for interpersonal relations, art, and politics. It ought to be a starting point for religious common ground. It ought to be the argument that saves the day when the peace talks break down. It should be welcome news to our ravaged self-confidence, our tattered solidarity. The image of God is saying: your worth is permanently guaranteed and protected. Self-hatred is a waste of time and energy. There are no spiritual haves and have-nots. Religion is not about esoteric knowledge to be hoarded by an elite and denied to others. The image of God is a human heritage. No one's been overlooked. The special dignity of the image of God—elusive, insistent, resistant to description, and that's as it should be—is a core intuition given to everyone.

I don't think I could write or teach or go to worship or face the day's thousand choices without somehow believing in the existence of the indwelling divine image. Every human encounter, every flash of eye contact, is haunted by the touch of God. Whenever I face a new group of writing students or poetry-retreat participants, I wonder at the propulsive circumstances that put us all in the room together at such a moment. Participants are there out of a need to create and express, or to find a less distorted relation to earth and sky and each other, or for reasons they can't explain. Perhaps it took an angelic entourage after all to herd everyone into the room, leaving everyone wide-eyed and a bit mystified at how we got here and what will happen next.

The notion of the image of God wasn't cooked up out of nowhere. It is spoken in Genesis 1:26, where God declares, "Let us make humanity in our image to resemble us." What does this mean? There's no agreement about it. According to one view, the image of God means we have qualities that we consider transcendent and God-like: reason, creativity, empathy, memory, self-awareness, a grasp of the future tense. Or, it means we are deputized as the Creator's representatives on earth, responsible for caring and paying attention on God's behalf.

Neither of these viewpoints gives people a free pass. The image of God isn't stamped on us like a coin with the face of the emperor, validating how great or saintly we are. Scholar Leon R. Kass offers a crucial cautionary argument. He points out that God in Genesis, after the various acts of creation, "saw that it was good"—but there are two exceptions. One is the firmament. The other is humankind. After neither of these acts of creation did God say "it was good."

Was the omission intentional? Kass argues that the human being's mark of the image of God implies a condition of unfinished potential, not finished perfection. Each person's freedom decides whether the image is embraced or squandered, for good or ill.

"A moment's reflection shows that man as he comes into the world is not yet good," he writes. "Precisely because he is the free being, he is also the incomplete or indeterminate being; what he becomes depends always (in part) on what he freely will choose to be. . . . It remains to be seen whether man will *become* good, whether he will be able to complete himself (or to be completed)."[2]

The New Testament also speaks about the image of God theme. The presence of Jesus overwhelms the old understandings, shifting the action to Jesus himself. He becomes the walking, talking image of the invisible God, God's presence on earth, according to Colossians. In the Gospel of John, Jesus invites people to look upon him and see the divine image, which then ricochets back onto the rest of us:

> If you have really known me, you will also know the
> Father. From now on you know him and have seen him.[3]
> Trust me when I say that I am in the Father and the
> Father is in me, or at least believe on account of the works
> themselves.[4]
> Remain in me, and I will remain in you. A branch
> can't produce fruit by itself, but must remain in the vine.
> Likewise, you can't produce fruit unless you remain in me.
> I am the vine; you are the branches. If you remain in me
> and I in you, then you will produce much fruit. Without
> me, you can't do anything.[5]

The way people experienced him rekindled their acquaintance with the ancient idea, an idea God put there. Without it, we'd have no detection equipment for relating to God. By decreeing that people populate the world, God made sure the image would circle the globe. "Where Mercy, Love, and Pity dwell / There God is dwelling too," says the William Blake poem.[6]

That's the idea, anyway.

Not everyone sees the world the way Blake does. The image of God remains a phrase of discomfort and evasion. The history of religion itself might be boiled down to conflicting attitudes toward the indwelling divine. Look at it as a sliding scale of zero to ten. Zero says there's no chance the human being is capable of carrying the image of God, while ten goes so far as to say we and God are identical if we'd just wake up to the fact.

The branches of Christianity of my acquaintance have drawn their own conclusions about the divine image, usually minimizing it or removing its glimmer by elevating our depravity—original sin— to solemn heights. In short, we don't deserve the image of God. We forfeited it, or damaged it beyond recognition, when we fled the original Garden as told in Genesis. Only faith in Jesus restores it.

All this gets unduly complicated. Daily experience itself is the best evidence and argument that human life is inscribed with qualities that aren't found elsewhere in nature—language, consciousness, the expression of prayer, despair, the dream of God and

> *Daily experience itself is the best evidence and argument that human life is inscribed with qualities that aren't found elsewhere in nature—language, consciousness, the expression of prayer, despair, the dream of God and paradise.*

paradise. There seems no escaping this condition of divine imaging. There's no use running from it. "The Kingdom of God is within," Jesus said. Such a thing couldn't be envisioned if the image of God weren't there already, like a synapse or an embedded poetry. It makes the moral imagination possible. Even when I'm in a fever of anger or angling for an ill-conceived advantage and the image of God is far from my calculations, the image keeps a piercing shimmer, waiting for acknowledgment.

Other things flow from this: the meaning of miracle shifts. If the image of God is an imprimatur, an imprint on each of us, then the great miracle has already happened. There's no need to force one out of the faith healer's TV show or scan the sky for a sign.

If the image of God is really imprinted on each person, then I can't accept it for myself alone and deny it in someone else.

The biblical idea of the image of God argues for the existence of life after death. The thought is: God would not destroy God's own image. God would not marginalize it or forget, even though that's what people are inclined to do. The divine image would, in fact, be safer in God's hands than ours. The afterlife is the repository.

If there were a local Congregation of the Image of God, that's what it would preach. There'd be readings from Genesis and the Gospels during public processions of dance and rhythm, a New Orleans-style second line. There'd be painting and pottery classes, neighborhood cleanup, and assistance to immigrants. There'd be no time for boastful political dividing lines.

All this makes me think of an old friend, writer Will Campbell, who died in 2013 after a life of doing battle against conventional wisdom, theological divisions, racial hatred, and concentrations of religious power. His unwavering theme was that God is reconciled with humanity already, through Jesus, and is now waiting for us all to own up to this fact and reconcile.

Campbell always short-circuited overbearing theological arguments by giving Christianity an eight-word definition: "We're all bastards but God loves us anyway."[7] Whether the image of God was bestowed on us in Genesis and survived the primordial Garden catastrophe, or whether it was shattered and needs repair, the groundwork for restoration is there. It's a matter of taking it up and laying down arms against ourselves and one another. Draw on the power of empathy. Dare to imagine that magnificence. Given the impressive record of human failings, this might sound glib or complacent. But even daring to imagine something better is a clue.

So this deeply enigmatic thing, the indwelling image, waits to be recognized and honored again, any moment now. That prospect ought to ease a bit the work of the angels, who stay impressively busy just ushering the image of God, by the billions, across the cosmos.

Chapter 12

SEASONS OF GOD:
Earth Tones

This year no kids appeared at the door demanding candy, but other characters in the Halloween night drama showed up as usual.

Jack-o'-lanterns gave off their weird charming glow throughout the neighborhood. The autumn leaves swirled along the streets. And, on cue, the evening wind heaved and gusted with a theatrical flourish, as if it knew this was paganism's New Year's Eve and it was time again to pay respects.

Amid bonfires, tricks, treats, and wild surmises about the great beyond, Halloween is an annual laboratory for the mingling of monotheism and polytheism: a temporary accommodation of faiths that vied for dominance for millennia. The holiday plays out around an ancient pagan notion that says the veil between the living and the dead was thinnest on the night of October 31. The earth itself—disdained by overly intellectualized philosophies, discounted by the surge of digital life—reasserts its place as a foremost spiritual stage once more.

That old drama still echoes intensely. People are yearning for connection—with one another, with God, with a usable and undistorted faith, with the love of loved ones passed, also with earth. Is God found within creation or outside it? Is earth sacred, or is it ours to exploit and despoil? Are we supposed to be stewards of creation or its dominators? Will digital revolutions demote earthy, earthly life to some inferior realm of existence, too slow for the glamour of high-def data delivery? Who's to say, and where is it written?

These questions define a modern fault line of belief. Much of the spiritual sorting out these days relates to one's attitude toward earth, and it usually tilts to one side or the other in distorted ways— either toward earth adoration or toward earth desecration. I know Christian believers who are suspicious of all hints of "secular" ecological earth-affection. I know erstwhile believers who have given up on church because it's hostile to earth care. They now take up a freelance form of earth worship in a sacred grove of the mind, using home altars and nature poetry as sanctuary and liturgy.

Now comes a third tendency. The digital life of screens is creating generations who feel extraordinarily stressed out by the pitiless speed of data and connectedness—overburdened by the pressure to keep up, the pressure to be exciting, the pressure to stay in front of the trends. The high-wire act of twenty-first-century life, teetering way above solid ground, traffics in the impatient thrill of instantaneous online entry, connection, and performance.

It's not a matter of condemning this new world. It's our world— vivid, mesmerizing, indispensable, fast. But there is power in naming what's challenging or peculiar about it, what it loses or disregards or retards. There's a need to take back our own power from the sleepless demanding stream of data. By reconnecting with the natural world—in the sharp glint of stone, fire, tree—the intuitions of the five senses bloom again.

One summer, on a remote and windswept rocky island across the sea, I placed my hands on a tall piece of stone that managed to reconcile these conflicts. The stone wasn't magical, nor was I in the market for a wizard who could heal the lesions in the Western mind. Yet there it stood, waiting at attention, sentry-like, with messages of its own. I was wandering the tiny historic isle of Iona, a spartan place of Christian pilgrimage and Celtic spirit off the west coast of Scotland, when I faced the famous stone cross outside the ancient church there.

The St. Martin cross, seventeen feet high, has been standing there for twelve hundred years. It has survived Viking invasion, doctrinal firestorm, the wild recurring seasons of twelve centuries of faith, doubt, and tempestuous weather.

I didn't know such a beautiful thing was there. What I did know was, I needed to touch it. Stone makes instant associations. It is material worthy of a church wall, a grave marker, a Ten Commandments tablet. Stone precedes us and outlasts us. It's like a solid silent link between earth and heaven, today and yesterday, God and us. The centuries had stormed upon the surfaces of this old Ionan cross, and it endured. Putting my hands on it was soothing. It felt warm in the sun. It felt like a homecoming.

The island of Iona has been a Christian outpost since the sixth century. From this spot, Celtic missionaries christianized Scotland. After many ups and downs, it is now enjoying a comeback as a beacon of Celtic spirituality. Sometimes one thousand people a week make pilgrimage. It's associated with meditative silence, love of nature, the power of grace, the mystery of the image of God deep within. It stands also for the practice of meditative Bible reading, the experience of sacred reading that awakens the core of one's own private hunches and longings.

As it's celebrated today, the Celtic brand of Christianity swerves around some of the brainier habits of western abstract thought in order to make contact with the poetry of belief. The Celtic sensibility feels at home on earth, letting stone and wind and harvest and human creativity make their own doctrinal statement under the sponsorship of Christ. This style of religious conviction is proving to be an attractive modern option, a way of catching up to what is awakening in many people—a hunger to reconnect with creation's eternal rhythms, a desire to make a difference in communal life, an impatience with the unfinished theological arguments of previous generations, a hunger to respond to the careening pluralistic world as they find it. The Celtic way is a firewalk, a path that pays fierce attention to night sounds, dreams, the arts, the senses, the innumerable shadows. A prayer from *Celtic Benediction: Morning and Night Prayer*, by J. Philip Newell, declares:

> You have given me eyes to see with, O God,
> and ears to hear life's sounds and sorrows
> and yet my seeing and hearing
> like my tasting and touching
> are wounded and weakened by failures.
> As rest can heal the sores of a body
> and sleep restores its strength

so may your angels of grace visit me in the night
that the senses of my soul may be born afresh.
Visit my dreams with messengers of grace, O God,
that the senses of my soul may be born again.[1]

I think the future of church depends on remembering a paradox of life on this planet: we experience time two ways at once.

One: we envision time marching on in a straight line to an end point. That's the logic of biblical monotheism: the Creator has in mind a beginning, middle, and end for the destiny of the cosmos.

Two: time also is cyclical. The seasons keep returning. The Sabbath reappears weekly. The sunrise is daily and necessary news.

This double perspective has the advantage of preserving respect for both Creator and creation.

Honoring a cyclical view of nature might, from the viewpoint of the theistic believer, conjure images of druids and sorcerers and pre-Christian practice. I think such suspicions fast become exaggerated and evasive. The obvious cycles of the year bring their own biblical news. I look forward to leaning out the window and taking in the changing seasons. They are immensely consoling. Each of them delivers cleansing agents and blessed relief.

Thus Halloween, an autumn highlight with its reveries in the key of orange, is a one-night curtain-raiser on a liturgical pageant that gets into gear in the fall and won't stop until the end of spring.

All Souls, All Saints, Thanksgiving . . . Before long, Christmas arrives

> *The future of church depends on remembering a paradox of life on this planet: we experience time two ways at once.*

and the world catches its breath for a minute. December's mercantile rush is over. The last-minute stuff got done, or it didn't. Society mislays its mask of bustle for a time. The nativity scenes are crowded with arrivals from the gospel story and will soon scatter again, sending shepherds and wise men to their open fields and mysterious roads home. Winter's season of cold is a time of alertness to seeking light, warmth, solidarity, journeying, and survival.

Just in time, spring brings the earth back to life, thawing out the senses and accompanied by momentous historical events that get renewed in congregational or family settings—Passover, Easter, Pentecost.

In summer, the church calendar takes a holiday. The season goes freestyle: baseball, beach, BBQ, Shakespeare in the park, heat, humidity, July 4, and rhubarb pie. The days burn long, until the signs slowly appear that the season's crazed green lushness is fading and fall will return again.

> O, how shall summer's honey breath hold out
> Against the wreckful siege of battering days,
> When rocks impregnable are not so stout,
> Nor gates of steel so strong, but Time decays?[2]

Insistently yet gently, the cyclical pull of the very universe orchestrates these seasonal transformations. The reliability of the annual cycle allows me to anticipate it. The cycle bids everyone to cherish the familiar, build memories, and trust the recurring fruits of the natural world. In these rituals—Easter egg hunt, autumn apple-picking, summer Sunday picnic—a person can make connections between the tiniest childhood memory and the vast movements of solar system and sun.

By comparison the twenty-first-century geopolitical world is frightfully unpredictable and getting more so. The changing seasons keep saying, at times loudly or quietly, that the whirling world of human artifice isn't built for the long haul. The bedrock of the created world is underfoot and unbudging.

The power of cyclical rhythms happens weekly, too, of course, though society is fast losing the memory of the sacred identity they've had. One Sunday morning recently, the neighborhood silence was shattered by a lawn-mowing crew that was working the house across the street. They buzzed the grass and clipped the hedges. They also mowed down an old taboo against making such a racket on the Sabbath.

It was 9 a.m. You aren't supposed to mow on Sunday morning! Everybody knows that, or used to. The sound had the grinding rumble of sacrilege. I thought about running out into the street to complain. But the work crew wasn't breaking any laws, except maybe something called the Fourth Commandment.

I don't propose a return to some Christian golden age. The mowing was a jarring violation of memory—the memory of Sunday rhythms of decades past—but Sabbath-keeping is not supposed to be an exercise in nostalgia. It is an imaginative response to the book of Genesis, the belief that God created all this, then rested and beheld the divine work. On the day God rested, I imagine the newly minted universe blazing forward at the speed of light in a blinding wall of atomic light, dark matter, and an in-dwelling sense of wonder. Our technology-centered life makes this experience of earth-and-sky astonishment more tenuous by the day, more remote by the hour.

The contemporary interest in alternative spiritualities is an attempt to find that connection again—reset a relationship between God and earth and us, heal body and soul, project a dream of goodness onto the damaged, dangerous big world. In the vessel of each person, the spirit brings potential light from across the far field. The alternative is everyone for himself alone in the dark, and annihilation isn't far away.

The sojourn of the spirit is a birthright. It deserves to come into its full inheritance without unmanageable mental strain. Arise and greet the seasonal transformations of creation, their companionship and scenic routes.

Chapter 13

SPEECH OF GOD:
Silent Partner

My only visit to Jerusalem was overscheduled and rushed, a crowded official tour for religion writers and journalists. But not everything was a blur. One moment I'll always remember: a Sabbath sunset that turned the ancient stones of the city to pink, then red, then ember gray, a sequence of colors unveiling the most awe-filled stillness I've ever known.

It was startling that the city of eternal truths and endless hostilities could turn so quiet. It was a Friday. Dusk was arriving, the beginning of the Jewish Sabbath. Traffic disappeared. I watched the last taxicabs of the day scamper away just as twilight descended. An old spell was cast. Under the cloudless sky the mystic night ship of Sabbath calm was docking into place.

This cosmic silence felt pre-existent. Many have imagined or proclaimed Jerusalem as the center of the world, even the center point of the beginning of creation, the first earthly thought that came to the mind of God. Legend has it that Adam himself was created on ground where Jerusalem sits. It seemed to me now that the city carried with it a recovered memory of the original stillness before those first explosive milliseconds of time and space.

Yet after a few minutes this silence unnerved me. It was hard to square the data: this municipal district mundanely shutting down for the weekend is also the birth canal for the world's three major monotheistic religions across thousands of years of apocalyptic claims and counterclaims.

Reports occasionally come out about pilgrims or travelers who go temporarily unhinged there, burning with biblical utterance, stripping off their clothes, declaring themselves to be God's next prophet or messiah announcing the end of time. They are reacting to the severities of the city's narrow lanes, the succession of centuries and conflicts. It gets to be too much to digest in mind and soul. Some people blow a fuse: it's called the Jerusalem Syndrome. They usually recover with some therapy, or simply by leaving the high-octane scene and going back home.

There's a certain pathological logic to it. The city's witness to sacred history, an inspiration to millions, is also vertigo-inducing, unsettling to the core. You can touch walls as old as Ezekiel and walk where the patriarchs of the Pentateuch walked, but behind it all is a depthless mystery—an abyss of silence, the enigma of God's original directives and God's refusal to say anything more. What we get instead, across the globe, is the daily noise of religious publicity, the fierce certainties of rival faiths, their violent literalisms, all of which ignore what lies beneath the human verbiage—a divine, pristine abstention from further speech. Is it God's absence, or a different form of presence?

The silence of the sacred stones can be unbearable. Outbreaks of Jerusalem Syndrome are, it seems to me, a rebellion against this. But they're also futile and self-centered, a rebellion against patience. The crazed logic says: better to break the silence and proclaim the details of Armageddon than take one's small place of respectful vigil before the heavenly mysteries.

Impatience is an underestimated force in religious history. When the divine silence refuses to break, we fill it ourselves, speaking for the Almighty, putting on the robes of heaven, improvising our own act of God, dragging God to our side (the "right" side) of an argument, and suddenly turning violent.

This is an attraction of cults. They dare to claim new revelation, a metaphysical breakthrough. God is speaking again—but only to them, giving them the code, speeding up the divine timetable, bending the rules just for them. They are connoisseurs of impatience.

The impatience happens daily in small ways or large. Here's one familiar path: Jesus said love your enemies. But surely he didn't mean Satan. We can't love *him*. Nor can we love the things of Satan (that much-cherished, ever-changing list: liberal know-it-alls, humanists, fundamentalists, communists, one-worlders, libertarians, heretics, and so on). What does it mean to love your enemy in a world of so many enemies? How is it done? Surely it's impossible. Surely it's not what Jesus meant. We already know who *our*

> *Impatience is an underestimated force in religious history. When the divine silence refuses to break, we fill it ourselves, speaking for the Almighty, putting on the robes of heaven, improvising our own act of God.*

enemies are. Therefore they are the enemies of Christ too. Therefore we'll speak for him. Which solves the problem of God's silence. The urgently dire state of the world, the argument goes, gives us leave to speak for heaven.

These contortions of certitude might be a sign of something else entirely—evidence of secret doubt, the dread that the divine silence points to divine absence, either God's unexplained desertion of the human scene or God's nonexistence in the first place.

Jerusalem threw me back into this old debate. That lovely sunset moment, blanketing the faith-drunk city, doubled as a warning—against spiritual greed. What the silence says to me is: You have what you need already. Stop asking for more. One way or another, divine revelation laid down sensible rules eons ago. The Lord has given us a road map—the Golden Rule, the Sermon on the Mount, the Four Noble Truths, the Five Pillars, the Eight-fold Path, the Ten Commandments—silent partners in the business of day-to-day living. Their moral coordinates keep the human race from destroying itself. We've made a mess of things by disregarding them.

Against the spiritual greed and pious violence done in the name of faith, I hear one of the great voices of scripture, a stout voice of opposition, Ecclesiastes: "Don't be quick with your mouth or say anything hastily before God, because God is in heaven, but you are on earth. Therefore, let your words be few."[1] What I hear is: accept the hiddenness of God as a great mercy. But know the Lord abides: "Worship God," Ecclesiastes concludes, "and keep God's commandments because this is what everyone must do."[2]

My fretful interior argument about silence relaxed a little when our tour bus hit the road again. We got out of town, leaving behind the politics, the sanctimony, and the fear of car bombs. We headed to Capernaum and Galilee.

The Sea of Galilee offered a different kind of quiet—serene rural images, the softened sunlight and gentle waves along the shoreline, the great backdrop to Jesus's emergence on the scene. These are good signs. In the annals of pathology, I know of no Galilee Syndrome.

The morning breeze and blue beauty of the lake had a mesmerizing effect. As our group stood along the shore, our Jewish guide did a lovely thing. He pulled out a New Testament and read aloud from the Gospel of John—the resurrection appearance at the lakeside, *this* lake, where the risen Christ is found awaiting his disciples and commences to grill some fish for their breakfast. The scene from John 21, unforgotten from so long ago, was delivered this time amid late-morning Galilean Technicolor:

> When they landed, they saw a fire there, with fish on it, and some bread. Jesus said to them, "Bring some of the fish that you've just caught." Simon Peter got up and pulled the net to shore. It was full of large fish, one hundred fifty-three of them. Yet the net hadn't torn, even with so many fish. Jesus said to them, "Come and have breakfast." None of the disciples could bring themselves to ask him, "Who are you?" They knew it was the Lord. Jesus came, took the bread, and gave it to them. He did the same with the fish. This was now the third time Jesus appeared to his disciples after he was raised from the dead. When they finished eating, Jesus asked Simon Peter, "Simon son of John, do you love me more than these?" Simon replied, "Yes, Lord, you know I love you." Jesus said to him, "Feed my

lambs." Jesus asked a second time, "Simon son of John, do you love me?" Simon replied, "Yes, Lord, you know I love you." Jesus said to him, "Take care of my sheep." He asked a third time, "Simon son of John, do you love me?" Peter was sad that Jesus asked him a third time, "Do you love me?" He replied, "Lord, you know everything; you know I love you." Jesus said to him, "Feed my sheep."[3]

Now the silence wasn't so lonely. Gathered there, our diverse group of Christians or skeptics or somewhere in between found we could share in the quiet and make a meal of it. The lapping water was a reassuring anchor, not a crisis of belief. The silence of God and the presence of God were no longer two different things. They were finding each other, merging, creating a signature, an indentation on soul and mind. What our guide did was a generous thing, bringing such words to bear at the famous shore.

All this was twenty-five years ago, yet the recollection is as vivid as ever. Returning home, I was removed again from Israel's burdensome history, the freeze-dried grievances that won't be laid aside—the unbearable contradictions, the conflicted dreams. But something was stamped on me at that moment of dusk in downtown Jerusalem. I heard a teaching coming from far outside me: God is present in this clearing away, this emptying of sound. When the error-prone human competition for truth is suspended for the moment and the night falls on the busy jamboree, it's not that we are instantly bereft, left with nothing. We are left with a space for getting some clarity about the divine nature. In such a space, a less distorted space, God stands by. I've been eager to get hold of that sort of silence again ever since.

Chapter 14

ENDURANCE OF GOD:
Known Unknown

The hometown church is 550 miles away these days, but I still carry inside me a tall, multicolored piece of the sanctuary front and center in the mystery temple of mind and heart.

It's a stained-glass panel depicting a familiar scene: Jesus serenely standing among a herd of sheep, holding a lamb. The image prevails like a still point through the fury of the passing decades.

The scene captures an essential metaphor of Christian life and history: Jesus the Lamb of God, Christ the Good Shepherd. But I see it first as a real moment in a real life—Jesus taking a break from the debates and the crowds, the harassed Son of Man stealing a moment with the happy company of small farm animals.

It's remarkable that such a memory was preserved in gospel history at all—that Jesus took time out during a brief, urgent public ministry to spend time with creation's wordless, pelt-skinned inhabitants. The moment bears a message: Jesus's circle of regard extends beyond human disputes over law and doctrine.

Surely the disciples were dismayed. It's no stretch to picture them pacing nearby, just outside the stained-glass frame, protesting: what an inefficient use of the Lord's time!

But there were lessons to learn from watching him with the sheep: self-forgetfulness, spontaneity, the genial flow of empathy with all the creatures of earth. The scene says: be ready for whatever comes next into view. Stay open. Grace and kinship may be found around the next corner.

Located behind the pulpit, this particular stained-glass scene towered over my boyhood Sabbath morns of vigilant or groggy prayer in the pew, during teen confirmation at the sanctuary altar, and also during the weekly benediction even when I was poised to make a fast getaway home for the noon NFL TV kickoff.

Wherever I am, memory holds this still-graceful panel, a fifty-year presence in the mind's eye. Whenever I make a worship visit there, I gravitate toward it. It telegraphs a message despite the grinding of the clock, despite changes in congregational demographics and the tenor of national politics and pluralism and fashions about God and religion and the changes in myself, too.

The stained-glass image resides as an unblinking eye inside time's hurricane, outlasting our fragmenting debates. I return to it as an indestructible image across shifting eras of giddiness and bewilderment.

The solidity of the image first came alive to me when I was a kid awakening to the noise and fascination of the 1960s, that national political-spiritual state of mind when "everything changed." By mid-decade, almost at once, trust in authority collapsed and commitment to old disciplines or customs fell away. Irreverence and sarcasm became the rage, a rage that only grows louder. The exact reasons for it all remain mysterious—probably a convergence of nuclear worry, Elvis worship, the trauma of World War II, post-colonial pluralism, more choices, more individualism, more mobility, more TV channels, more everything.

The turmoil continues. I can feel the winds kicking up—the way churches get caught in the crossfire of society's conflicts over race, gender, war, class, economics, technology, weekend priorities, and entertainment: the church ever in transition, second-guessed, under siege. Now as ever, the nonreligious world rumbles along on its own terms, indifferent to belief or unable to comprehend it, as if thirty-five hundred years of religious tradition never happened or never made civilization possible. There's a party going on—elsewhere.

Yet the image of Jesus is there to keep me circling back to first principles—scripture, sacraments, memory, hope, action—despite the noise machine, despite tumultuous past and uncertain future. Conjuring the stained-glass silent Jesus with the flock of sheep, I feel a rebuke. I get the lingering impression that the figure in the glass panel isn't particularly impressed by any thumbnail argument of cultural decline or doctrinal triumphalism or self-pity. He's quite literally unmoved, as if underwhelmed by it all. The day's many psychodramas aren't as awesome as we think. The baseline of human nature didn't change after Woodstock, Vietnam, Watergate, Reaganomics, terrorism, globalization, climate change, and whatever was hot this morning in social media. The condition of the invisible God hasn't changed either. The Ten Commandments are still there to be tried someday. The Sermon on the Mount remains on file.

Another condition hasn't changed: the freedom of one person to sit still, while all around the bristling disagreements fly and the divisions crackle. I make a living by words, by the hunt for as many angles on an argument as possible, but the stained-glass window showed me something different: here was Jesus, returning once again, not requiring wordy rhetoric, just inviting attention to the dispatches that are tapping away inside the heart, ready for release.

Rowan Williams, former Archbishop of Canterbury, has written about the power of icons, how they function as a borderland, a transitional place between the foreign and the familiar, to make us aware that the power of God waits in the core of what's real before our eyes—"as if the world were always on the edge of some total revolution, pregnant with a different kind of life, and we were always trying to catch the blinding momentary light of its changing. That is what any icon sets out to embody and transmit."[1]

Neither in artistic style nor liturgical function is the stained-glass image a classic icon. But it has its effect on me. The point is to be a welcoming party to it in the present moment. Postpone other pressing business and await further instructions. It's no great leap to think some unexpected word of reconciliation will come. A Holy Spirit operation? It happens all the time.

To my surprise, a certain clutter is stripped away. The distortions of history yield the floor. To my surprise, it's possible to step out from under the burden of today's care and imagine something refreshing. It's a knight move off the chessboard, suspended momentarily in the air until it lands again, at an angle. The rules allow it. The rules sponsor it.

This effect of an artistic image of Jesus happens despite a certain irony: the New Testament gives no physical description of Jesus. That was a brilliant move. Imagine if a convincing composite sketch had survived. Imagine the millions who would alter their appearance just to look like him and forget their own identities. Imagine the massive institutional attempts to capture his look in 3-D and not his words.

More than a century ago the German theologian/missionary Albert Schweitzer torpedoed the hope that the search for definitive details of the historical Jesus was still possible. Those details are beyond recovery, unknowable. We project our own theories and anxieties onto the elusive figure. Schweitzer declared we should face a great simple truth and act on it. What we have are not physical descriptions of the redeemer but something more potent, his words: "Follow me."

"He comes to us as one unknown, without a name, as of old, by the lakeside, he came to those men who did not know who he was," Schweitzer wrote. "He says the same words, 'Follow me!' and sets us to those tasks which He must fulfill in our time. He commands. And to those who harken to him, whether wise or unwise, he will reveal himself in the peace, the labors, the conflicts and the sufferings that they may experience in his fellowship, and as an ineffable mystery they will learn who he is."

Any stained-glass portrait is nothing more than one artist's idea of the Christ. Nevertheless, such depictions, no matter how varied, stay focused on a basic fact: the human figure of Jesus was embedded in real-world noise and need, gravity and grit. Someone out of scripture, whatever he looked like, walked into history.

Stained glass doesn't magically conjure the presence of God. But there is something sacred about giving space to the soul so it can breathe and repair.

There's nothing sacred about stained glass, stone arches, candlelight, and wooden pews. I've visited windowless worship auditoriums, strip-mall church meetings, and tent revivals where the holy bursts through. No, stained glass doesn't magically conjure the presence of God. But there is something sacred about giving space to the soul so it can breathe and repair. Grandeur, reverence, beauty, and silence are not the marks of some musty worship style that the 1960s swept away. Those things are a fixed condition of human need across the ages. Without them, I wither and flatten. The headstrong passing parade of history is brilliant, exhausting, reckless, half-crazy. It's also fickle. The claim of belief is not. Every new day is the next page in the world's unwritten history, our allotted moment to engage and confront it.

That's what a church with its beckoning art should inspire when you sit down inside a sanctuary or assembly hall or approach a labyrinth or stone altar—the long view, a consoling sanity, a renewed search for the undistorted God.

So, following the stained glass, my eye moves through countryside and herds of sheep, through writhing town and danger. It watches the changing colors of light in the unchanging mystery temple.

Chapter 15

GEOGRAPHY OF GOD:
Going Places

Everybody knows places that are infused with a religious mood. Specific theologies attend landscapes. There is such a thing as spiritual geography.

Stepping into a Kansas wheat field puts me right away into the climate of the book of Ecclesiastes. The endless wind, the golden beauty, the farmer humility in the face of the unpredictable weather—these things speak to Ecclesiastes's skepticism about human pretensions and his affirmation of the unstoppable sovereignty of God.

Hurrying along the streets of midtown Manhattan, I feel thrown into a very different atmosphere: a modern staging of the Acts of the Apostles, that New Testament record of the early Christian movement amid the teeming cities of the Roman Empire. I hear the global tongues. I see the skyscraping monuments to imperial ambition. Jostling with the multitude of passersby, I surmise secret spiritual yearnings amid epic material strivings and unknown gods.

Visiting the still deserts of the Holy Land, I can understand why it was home to monotheism's first convulsive revelations. The uncompromising emptiness brought news that found its way into the Pentateuch: God will not be reduced to familiar images or convenient local habitations. Humans will have to reckon with this Creator on the Creator's terms.

Yes, the spirit of landscape attends one's every step on solid earth. I grew up in Louisiana, went to college on the Great Plains and to graduate school in Nashville, and lived in recent years in New England—all different landscapes, all different windows on God.

Studies bear out this diversity. Scholars at Baylor University, for instance, found that Americans can be divided over four basic different images of the Lord.[1] They are:

1. Authoritative God, who is engaged in the world and judges it. (This one is most popular in the South.)
2. Benevolent God, who is engaged but not judgmental. (This one is favored in the Midwest.)
3. Critical God, who is unengaged but judgmental. (This one is most recognized in the Northeast.)
4. Distant God, who is neither engaged nor judgmental. (The region that favors this one is the West.)

This is no parlor game or intellectual exercise. Our working understandings of God—and our disagreements over them—dictate different denominational styles, social goals, ideological divisions, and attitudes about the future, whether hopeful or pessimistic. Is God majestic and distant, or close and intimate? Every landscape and homeland will trigger a different outlook and memory. Each place is a gift of discovery. Yet each also represents a temptation to absolutize only what's familiar and turn God into merely a local deity.

Regional identities and personal quirks create a profusion of divine images. Multiply this pluralistic impulse by seven billion earthlings and the result is, at the extremes, explosive global conflict. Trouble comes when I think the spiritual style of my particular place deserves the final word, customizing who God is and who I am and who you are as friend or enemy. At issue is the need to grapple with the power of landscape to shape religious feeling or distort it. This is a personal challenge and an international one. At stake is a society of war or peace.

An undistorted monotheism turns away from the assured claims of any one group's slanted relationship to divine truths. A decluttered faith is wary of nonreligious factors—political, economic, class-oriented—that contort religious identities. It seeks a bigger unity behind all the shards and perspectives, gathered from miles or hemispheres away.

Is that possible?

One of my first apprehensions of God was also an early scary memory during a visit with Kansas relatives: waiting out a fierce thunderstorm in the family farmhouse late one night on the western plains. Off in the great distant darkness, a long prong of lightning suddenly struck the ground, followed by the shattering thunder. At age five, clutching the bedsheet, I screamed. It looked to me like the bright skeletal fingers of God coming down to scorch the defenseless surface of the earth. It took several rounds of the hymn "All Things Bright

111

and Beautiful" at church the next morning to return me to a more benign view of divine purposes. Years later I learned that an uncle on the farm, as a young boy, had been killed by lightning on this same acreage, just over the hill. It was of course a lasting family sorrow. The savage power of nature, the challenges to faith—the abundance and enigma of God—were never far from ancestral memory.

My experience reveals every region throbbing with spiritual information. Living in Connecticut for several years, I could sense the afterglow and half-life of Puritan heritage, mixed in with the daily ambitions of the propulsive Eastern Seaboard corridor, a stoicism about the snow and wind, as well as a common-sense regard for the religious pluralism that has accumulated with every new wave of immigration for the last two hundred years.

In Tennessee, where I live now, I can witness the gentle rhythms of weekly churchgoing as well as the latest surge of political Christianity—also, in certain quarters, a rising indifference to the old habits of faith, as well as a youthful exuberance about retelling the gospel story to new generations. Outside Nashville you can see thousand-year-old Indian mounds that remind the bustling twenty-first-century denizen of the passing of all civilizations, the changing ways of talking to God.

The geography of spiritual mood—the menu of divine images—isn't restricted to sectional grids on the map. It governs internal landscapes. Family history and parental style—whether an environment of encouragement, judgmentalism, or absence—help shape one's God-odyssey. Atheists are not exempt. As I hear it argued, atheism stays busy rejecting a particular sort of God, perhaps based on a bad experience in a religious institution back in childhood.

My father came from Arkansas, my mother from Kansas. Their own upbringing was Calvinist and Lutheran, respectively, the meat of the Reformation lineup. I came along and absorbed it all but then gravitated toward the worship style of Anglicanism, with its regular weekly Eucharist, which was a revelation to me when I first discovered it during a teenage trip to England. This arc of personal memory—Wesleyan hymns, sovereignty of God, *Book of Common Prayer*—defines an inward spiritual horizon even as I remain a free-floating vessel on post-Protestant seas.

These compulsive inner horizons and their real-time epiphanies reveal themselves around the dinner table. Especially there. I once dampened a perfectly good late-night discussion about God among a group of colleagues. We were modestly weighing in on the old, impenetrable mysteries. Yet our thoughts about God seemed to go according to the sort of week everyone was having—God as the Santa Claus of blessing, God the disappointment, or God the trickster. One friend said his new job was sailing along fine; all was well with the Lord. Another was feeling dejected about the lack of a boyfriend and dour about the possibility that God exists.

It was sounding as if belief is automatically tied to circumstance and mood, as if the reality of God depended on the work status and social successes of a few locals huddled together in one corner of one town in one state of one country on one continent in one hemisphere of one planet in one solar system of one known universe.

I blurted out: "God exists whether I'm in the mood this week to believe

> *I blurted out: "God exists whether I'm in the mood this week to believe God exists or not."*

113

God exists or not." That didn't settle anything, naturally, but they had said their piece and now I said mine, planting a flag against the fickle dictatorship of my day-to-day emotions. There's a daily tendency to fashion God into just one thing, whether Judge or Eternal Light or Father or Unconditioned Unknowable or more likely the promoter of my own agenda. So much for the sophisticated modern mind.

One honored solution to this cacophony is to empty the head of all divine images by the discipline of eyes-shut meditation. Make contact with the true God beyond the word *God*, beyond the constructs and accidents of words. I've never been good at that. (Neither will my attempts at yoga impress anybody.) My angle on this waking life is: keep eyes and ears open. Otherwise I might miss something.

The Bible, as it turns out, preserves a sly truth. It refuses to settle on one divine image. It is an unblinking, unapologetic repository and record of the many projects of God. It reflects the changing geographic or historical circumstances of the writers who recorded its stories, poetry, parables, and chronologies—medleys of hospitable or fearsome images, all claiming space, rubbing up against one another. Creator, avenger, healer, rock, lamb, king, shepherd, shield, flame, protector, eagle, bear, comforting mother—they are all found residing in the Bible's noisy boardinghouse of images and messages. That seems to be the point: it takes the whole Bible to get the full picture, a fuller one than I am willing to carry around. The aim is not to pick and choose among them but quiet down and let them all speak, each in its moment. The slow drip of scripture, its cocktail of ingredients and enzymes, finds the bloodstream.

This description of the biblical record might sound like a crisis—too many images, a havoc of tongues, a sign of bewilderment. But I prefer it. The clustered concordance and discordance of Bible and tradition subvert any claim of permanent or overly confident grasp of divine power. The undistorted God slips free of the anvil weight of exaggerated images, the exploitation by ideologues.

My favorite spot on the spiritual map is in a lawn chair under the biggest sky I can find, wherever I am. It helps to keep a notebook nearby: thoughts can unspool and I try to confront whatever twitchy unresolved emotions are weighing me down. At such a moment, landscape and inner-scape meet on the horizontal lines of a page. Phrases or dreams or prejudices I didn't know I was stowing away, hidden and unbidden until now, come out of the dark. They are demystified. For a while, I feel liberated from the tyranny of the local.

Franz Kafka once spoke to the immense potential of one's own tiny latitudes of perception no matter where one is on earth: "Life is as infinitely great and profound as the immensity of the stars above us. One can only look at it through the arrow keyhole of one's personal existence. But through it one perceives more than one can see. So above all one must keep the keyhole clean."[2]

The billion faces and places of creation offer their own habitations of intuition and poetry. But there's usually a slant to the local lay of the land, a parochial distortion. Scripture's witness offers a teeming dissent, a swift-moving divine force that cannot be imprisoned or silenced by the accidents of hometown terrain or the passing fashions of media or my own fly-by-night elations.

> *My favorite spot on the spiritual map is in a lawn chair under the biggest sky I can find, wherever I am.*

The Almighty won't fit on a bumper sticker or questionnaire or worship bulletin. Better the composite sketch of biblical record—divine anger, love, withdrawal, action, promise, puzzle, abiding—than any argument that I or anyone else happens to bring in out of the rain, wind, and tumult of personal geography.

Chapter 16

VIGIL OF GOD:
Monastery Confidential

L ittle outbreaks of peace come without warning. After staying a few days in a monastery, I got the idea to write a letter to God. It took a while to get started. I hadn't done such a thing before, and it seemed at first like a stunt and God would be onto it. But I wanted to discipline my wandering mind. I wanted to hold my thoughts accountable so that a written letter, or the spirit of the Lord, would reveal them or expose them no matter how half-baked.

I imagine other guests that week were trying their own off-center experiments in prayer or transparency. We had sought out this rural monastic location and welcomed its temporary severity as a corrective to some harassing force in our lives, an attempt to master destructive impulses, or just get a moment's rest.

I brought my own anxieties about relationships, family, and career. It's impossible to leave all that behind. I had to learn to shift away from the x-ray self-scrutiny, molt off some of the old skin (the frets, regrets, and to-do lists), and just listen for what might come next, what phrases or directives. Elemental forces rule the monastic routine at all hours—silence, prayers, soup and bread for a meal. These conditions gave me a window on my own buried thoughts swiftly rising—weather forces tapping at my window that I don't usually stop to hear.

In the Dear God letter I tried to speak without self-consciousness. Stand before the living God. Ask questions, hazard surmises, express gratitude: pour a prayer onto paper. I had no idea how it would go from there.

> *Dear God:*
>
> *I've never tried this kind of thing before (as you know). But I believe in your patience. I believe your patience includes waiting for me to one day understand my own heart and finally catch wind of your intentions on this green and mysterious planet.*
>
> *The philosophers' old question persists: why is there anything rather than nothing? I take it that the answer is self-evident: because you decided. I walk around, often stupefied, at what there is to see: life itself, life at all, this astonishing fact. This world is your answer to whatever the question is. I want to carry the love of that answer in my bones to the end, if there must be an end.*
>
> *So much is going wrong—the world situation, the damage, our insincerity about making peace, our trust in violence and racism, your name used in vain. My thoughtless actions and inactions—I can't excuse them. But your patience, I believe, reveals parental watchfulness*

and also faith, if I can say that—your faith in us that
someday, maybe today, we'll begin to turn things around.
That we'll choose to be less miserable.

Bible, tradition, poetry, worship, good works—these
are coordinates. They are the walls of a house, the invisible house I sit in now, a place of solidity and, for the
moment, quiet—the dwelling place of your presence. It
holds us by your effortless concentration, the hidden nuts
and bolts of the universe, laws of your choosing, forces
that sustain everything.

Not for a second do I know what I'm doing or what
you're doing. Did the Bible stories get all the details right?
I no longer agonize about it. I take them to mean they
could have happened that way because you have the power
to make them happen. The stories are a memory and an
announcement of that power.

Ecclesiastes said you "placed eternity" in our hearts.
That eternity is what I pursue. It pursues everyone.

Billions sense you nearby, other billions reportedly
don't. This is the great puzzle. I can't fathom the num-
bers and ratios, the distribution of blessing. I think of the
millions and millions dead—Jewish children under the
Nazis, the thousands everywhere this morning, perishing
after terrible pain. I'm suddenly on the edge of a cliff,
the abyss of ignorance. Why must evil keep coming and
coming? Why cancer . . . schizophrenia . . . tsunamis?
Questions. In heaven's name, may everyone find security

in your care. "Cast me not away from thy presence; and take not thy holy spirit from me" (Psalm 51:11 KJV).

The soul meanwhile has its standing orders. It's on duty. So I am praying. I pray for my neighbors:

For the Muslim family across the way: may there be friendship between us.

For my loved ones far-flung.

For the armies of the world. For mercy on their victims.

My faith is in the miraculous prospect that acceptable words will ship out to some unmapped dimension and be received. Here we all are, equipped to make our way into that open space . . . and find solidarity with divine purpose . . . and make alliance with each other, if we dare.

Caution says I ought to shut down this letter and hit delete. Except that you gave us skill to communicate. This was your doing, these modes of transport to your door. I hope to shed as many foolish private distortions as possible until I'm down to one possession: a true identity.

It is a beautiful afternoon out. I am grateful for people, for marriage, for work, for solutions, for self-forgetfulness, for color and light, for the English language, for sleep. Amen.

Journal entries during my monastery visit provided the first rough draft of some surprising thoughts. Monastic rigor even for a few days has a way of stripping your life to a nearly blank page. There's nowhere to hide in a place shorn of excess, affluence, and media options. So you write things down. You get out from under old routines. You begin to begin again, a new adventure.

Time thickens and slows there. I read, ate, and walked more deliberately. Slowing down, I was trying to catch up to something. An unexpected rhythm sunk in. We monastery guests were invited to become innkeepers to a new creativity, a new guest, in each of us.

The 3:00 a.m. nightly service was a turning point. I left my small guest room of cinder block and single bed, my plain cell bereft of TV, Wi-Fi, and excuses, and joined thirty other guests for this wee-hours Vigils (or Matins) liturgy, where fifty monks were already gathered without fanfare. We staggered into the gallery as the monks sang psalms, then our shy voices joined theirs during their prayers for the world. Vigils is the night watch hour, the appointed time to greet the deep dead of night.

This headachy, early-morning time slot was never Christianity's finest hour, not in the beginning. In the Gospel accounts it was this time of night, before the rooster crowed, that Peter denied Jesus in the teeth of the accusatory crowd. Now the blackened hour is being reclaimed and refurbished—a sort of penance, probation, community service.

It's not to be taken for granted. Much is at stake. We're not usually taught to make a dance partner of dark shadows. But such odd-hour operations at a monastery argue that God is awake and at work even if we are not: the inconceivable intricacies of divine management of the cosmos go on day and night no matter how inconvenient the hour. These worship services, seven a day, are a way of keeping a bright candle lit for the Creator of us all. Keep a vigil. Write a letter. See if anything happens next.

The monks witness to this idea of keeping the flame of soul-making alive. They stay busy with manual labor and worship every day, year in and out, plowing and clearing the field of being. In their routines I saw something freeing, a joy taken in their chores, their good fortune of discovering their vocation, and now a delight in offering a sliver of it to us overfed, over-stressed outsiders.

One night after supper, one of the monks offered a little talk to the guests, a sermon mixed with snippets of nineteenth-century poetry. He said God is not present to our habits of hatred and darkness—bigotry, cruelty, neglect of each other. Those things are people's own doing, not God's. Those things keep the light from streaming in. We can change that at any time. We have the power to keep the light burning in the present instant.

With that the homiletic monk finished, releasing us like happy balloons back to our little rooms. One thing was there in my cell to greet me—the sound of my own breathing, in a new space of freedom.

That final evening, I stopped in the courtyard where there's a sign above the gate: "God Alone." I lingered there, admiring the phrase's lack of clutter, a theology in two words. I mentally played with a few variations. God (is) Alone. (Leave) God Alone. (Try Giving Attention to) God Alone. I ended up with God Alone (Prevails). Commit to that idea, and look for a gift left at the doorstep, a gift of purpose and propulsion.

> *That final evening, I stopped in the courtyard where there's a sign above the gate: "God Alone." I lingered there, admiring the phrase's lack of clutter, a theology in two words.*

After just a few days, my monastic time was up. I'm not a monastery junkie, returning again and again. If I want a shot of monastic essence, I read Thomas Merton's journals, which weave devotional thoughts, theological whims, and sketches of his everyday life (sometimes his frustrations) as a Roman Catholic Trappist monk. The point is not to be anxious about leaving this womb of serenity. The better idea is to take some slice of it with me. Reshape personal conditions for the pursuit of divine contemplation or commitment. Keep the adventure going.

D. H. Lawrence once wrote a remarkable short essay in which he roughed out a history of humanity based on the species' one irrepressible trait: we are "thought adventurers." Civilization makes advances on the courage of small groups—arks—of people who keep the illuminated spirit going during ages of chaos. Monasteries were little arks that kept prayer and practice alive in the uncertain centuries of the first Christian millennium.

"The monks and bishops of the early Church carried the soul and spirit of man unbroken, unabated, undiminished over the howling flood of the Dark Ages," Lawrence wrote. "Then this spirit of undying courage was fused into the barbarians, in Gaul, in Italy, and the new Europe began. But the germ had never been allowed to die. . . . If I had lived in the year four hundred, pray God I should have been a true and passionate Christian. The adventurer."[1]

Lawrence, writing in 1924, thought Christianity was done for: the moral bankruptcy and carnage of World War I had discredited Western religion, which embraced the war from the opening shot. No, he declared: it was time for a new venture toward God.

As prophecy, Lawrence was mistaken, or at least hasty and impatient. The gospel adventure toward God continues. The ark floating on the blind, roaring sea still carries the freight of truth-seeking, peace-making, and incarnation toward God. A monastery visit confirms it. So does the work of a million churches.

Driving home the next day, a ninety-mile trip, new words came to me, a poem, a valentine for a special place:

We guests took in the barnyard tour
and saw a sinewy monk or two
before guestmaster left us to our lunch.
Beneath the no-talking sign the only sound
was my pocket daily planner snug in my vest,
rattling its facts. I sat down to silence,
my new dinner partner, who had been waiting
politely there forty years for such a moment.

The monks get up at 3 a.m. and head
to the sanctuary while everyone else trudges
through muggy weather of dreams and
second thoughts. I followed them to worship
—a stunt to tell back home—but sat agape
to watch them at their chapel prayers,
the night shift taking its turn, renewing the
fierce lobby of faith at invisibility's door.

On our last night, I took a wrong turn down
the monks' dimmed hallway.
Before guestmaster could shoo me off,

I saw them all returning slowly to their cells
after another spent round of Psalms.
Seen and unseen, the monks carry their silence
like a candle that won't go out.
Lit for the roaming heart of earth,
their candle burns away clean and bright.

I'm still revising the letter to God, adding sections, because there's never a final version. This life itself is one continuous draft— edited, altered, and (I hope) improved on until the final deadline.

Chapter 17

FEAR OF GOD:
Burning Light

O nce upon a time, people drove cars that had names like vacation spots and exotic locales—Bel Air, Monte Carlo, Catalina, Biscayne. Drivers had destinations in mind. They'd seen the colorful travel brochures. They knew where they wanted to go.

Soon came a shift. People were stepping into Pathfinders, Explorers, Odysseys, Escapes, and Outlanders. The inner life was changing, launching the soul on a new kind of odyssey, an open-ended quest without the usual maps and guidebooks, destination unknown.

I first heard the "quest culture" described this way in 2000 by sociologist Wade Clark Roof.[1] I loved him for that—his marvelous attention to the names of car models as a spiritual sign of the times. It's why I got into the writing trade—to observe such shifts, make connections, sift through the permanent and impermanent, figure out where God might be in all this, how we get it right or get it wrong and why.

At times, this has brought me to great perplexity—not anxiety that God is absent, but the odd impression that God is talking too much.

The range of claims about Jesus, miracles, school prayer, denominational truth, war, and peace looked unseemly. The many-splintered arguments among believers, all quoting scripture, seemed to put God in a tight spot, implying that the Almighty is blessing a cavalcade of chaos or stands indifferent to helping any of us get discernment on how to live. Does God love war or hate war? Does God want to save the world or destroy it? Does God bless all people or only a narrow caliber of credentialed believers? The petitioners leave a mess of mixed signals and distorted religion that they never clean up.

I wondered why God would so poorly equip us for reaching consensus. We mangle and multiply the arguments, divide humanity into seething camps. People finally get tired of this. In my newsroom days, I heard from readers who complained to me that my daily reports were delivering too many competing arguments and angles on a religious controversy. Just tell us the truth, one reader demanded over the phone one morning, as if I was withholding official illumination of heaven, refusing to share. What he was really saying was he too was weary of the clutter and the distortions.

In such a climate, a lot of exasperated people have simply given up on religion. They made a shift. They now get their moral passion from politics instead—from a politicized version of their religion, creatively misquoting scripture to shore up electoral rage. Ideological commentary—selective data, pseudo experts—supplies people with purpose and resentment, eclipsing the old religious teachings about empathy, forgiveness, and change of heart. Mutual trust is in decline.[2]

Many such people used to connect with congregational life, where they discovered a personal place in a providential universe and a specific duty to the Golden Rule. Healthy religion inspired personal restraint, business integrity, and public truthfulness. *People believed God was watching.*

I was in a cab the other day, and the driver was happy to talk. He told me he's a former alcoholic who had been prone to violence. Now he's a churchgoer peaceably submitting to biblical regulation, which crushes the old destructive impulses and regrets.

"This is my protection now," he said, pointing to a big leather Bible crammed on the dashboard near the meter.

"In the past, I was ready with a knife. One time, I crouched all night, waiting for my enemy. Luckily he never came. Today it's simple. I give it all up to God. It says so in this Holy Bible: fear of the Lord is the beginning of wisdom."

I gazed out the window, his words echoing: fear of the Lord. Despite every burden and complication, every refusal, maybe life is that simple after all. Salute the overpowering divine reality, stand down the monstrous impulses of the self, and live.

"Fear of the Lord"—not a fashionable idea these days. It smacks of the old franchise of abusive religious guilt and manipulation. The culture has shifted and left it behind.

But the phrase still has value, if it registers a basic existential fact—a measure of the gap between Creator and creatures in every generation. The creature reaction need not be trembling gloom but charity, clarity, and awe.

The cabbie gets his inspiration from the old book with the stubborn title: Holy Bible. That name still fascinates. Its persistence through the centuries preoccupies even the nonbeliever. Its sheer lumbering uncoolness adds to its power. It stands like a monument in a constant sandstorm.

Taking a break from e-mail and the rest of it recently, I did the most un-digital, the least 2.0 thing imaginable. I read the Old Testament's book of Proverbs, that sober cascade of biblical instruction for living. Proverbs is sometimes wordy or repetitive, but its meaning rings clear enough: seek God's care and find well-being, or turn away and watch your life fall apart.

A life of abundance, it says, depends on self-restraint, simplicity, consideration of others, a dose of humility. Let these God-engineered things enter your heart, and "knowledge will be pleasant in your soul," and "discretion will protect you." Avoid those things that insult God—lies, haughtiness, false witness, wicked schemes, the shedding of innocent blood. The Ten Commandments pretty much cover the list.

There ought to be a way to regard the humane vision of scripture not as a tract for justifying a political position but as a force for repositioning oneself in the cosmos. We don't get this from, say, the conversation around technology. The exuberant logic of the technological future says: there are no limits. What is newest and fastest prevails, and let's not worry about the consequences until later. The database of faith says something different: we are not limitless God-like avatars. Maturity comes with the knowledge that we are beholden to a divine force larger than we can control. Denying this, we will destroy ourselves.

The tone of this proverbial advice, its confidence and gravitational force, keeps me staring at the printed page.

Taking a break from e-mail and the rest of it recently, I did the most un-digital, the least 2.0 thing imaginable. I read the Old Testament's book of Proverbs, that sober cascade of biblical instruction for living.

Scripture's many voices and tones, singing out across the riot of centuries, create heat and friction. My experience of this relies not on a well-turned argument about biblical authority but on an encounter with the text itself, unvarnished, unrehearsed, in my own interior secret chamber or in the congregational round at worship time. The friction generates a glow—the light of the embers of some original pillar of fire.

This, if anything, is what it means to say scripture is sacred. People can ignore it, explain it away, denounce it, misread it, suppress or domesticate it, but the glow won't dim. It has its say and moves in whatever direction it will next. Otherwise the Bible belongs in the literature section only, a Bronze Age curiosity for comparative religion class and comedy-club jokes. Bluesman Blind Willie Johnson, in his song "Soul of a Man," offers an affectionate theological riff. The Bible? "It's nothing but a burning light,"[3] he declares after years of reading and pondering.

More than a century ago, many believers sensed the dynamism of God and read the Bible, not with glum foreboding, but with care and hopefulness. A cultural shift engaged biblical imagination: the Bible was pored over as a corrective message to contemporary conditions, and the result was a social reform movement that improved labor, housing, and educational standards for millions. The Social Gospel movement dreamed of a partnership with the Almighty based on the example of the Prince of Peace. Fear of the Lord implied something positive, a sense of responsibility for social improvement, a ministry to body and soul, not despair that God was angrily unappeasable.

The twentieth century's grinding sorrows of war and mass murder and assassination became the chief cultural experience and memory, and the Social Gospel movement was depleted.

Martin Luther King Jr., sparked by the language of the biblical prophets, was the last to bring the Social Gospel vigor and hope to the scene.[4] It enriched his Christian politics, making him a world citizen, expanding his outlook on human rights and economic justice and gospel values. When he was murdered in Memphis in 1968, a trajectory of religious hope was shot down. In the decades that followed, public life has been awash with suspicion, marked by pledges of allegiance to ruthless power and bloodlust, leavened by private fantasies of fame and riches. In the minds of many, religion has settled for violent apocalypse as the only future worth imagining.

No movement is permanent, not even the bitter metallic taste of pessimism. Humane breakthroughs still happen because civilization still remembers ideals as old as biblical tradition—love of neighbor, the God who cares about human history, the eternal value placed on every human soul because everyone is made in the image of God.

"An undercurrent of optimism still exists in America," writer-educator Earl Shorris declares. "There is an American sermon to deliver on the unholiness of pessimism."[5]

The Bible tests and scandalizes and pushes a reader to declare a response. Proof of biblical authority today might simply come down to this: it happens whenever the text compels a person, despite all sociological predictions, to power down all devices so its voice can make its case. In this way God invites human involvement. Wisdom is not a set of marbled rigid certitudes memorized and rehearsed but a train of practical logic, applicable by the hour and eliciting the heat of inquiry.

"Conflicts, struggles and contradictions within the Bible also witness to its authority," writes Phyllis Trible. "The book teems with life, promotes dialogue, and resists platitudes."[6]

Some argue that "fear of the Lord" in the Bible is better rendered as awe or dread or trembling adoration: it's a way of marking our "uneasy conscience and divided loyalties."[7] Fear describes the moral distance between God and humanity. But that distance is shortened by the texts that come down the ages. They survive because they transfer heat from page to reader, from past to present, perhaps from heaven to earth.

And a new experience happens. It's no longer fear, or only fear. An invitation is privately tendered, whispered. Poet Richard Howard says the Bible keeps prodding—and keeps selling—because it carries an elusive secret: "Because on every page in every line, it hints at something that it does not reveal but that tempts us, arrests us, fascinates us all the more . . . the secret is that Scripture is addressed not to everyone but to each one, not to the public but to the individual."[8]

Proverbs 30, a plea to God, is a remarkable bundle of sobriety, affection, and pragmatism. It patiently waits, perhaps hundreds of years at a time for the right moment, the next reader:

> Two things I ask of you;
> don't keep them from me before I die:
> Fraud and lies—
> keep far from me!
> Don't give me either poverty or wealth;
> give me just the food I need.
>
> Or I'll be full and deny you,
> and say, "Who is the Lord?"

> Or I'll be poor and steal,
> and dishonor my God's name.[9]

I can imagine this sounded like a foundational goal of civilization when it was written some twenty-three hundred years ago. Centuries later, it still burns a hole of light in the darkness.

Chapter 18

POWER OF GOD:
Eucharist Revisited

The last time I prayed with raw desperation was at midnight during a storm a couple of years ago: a hurricane was heading toward us and ready to hit by daybreak. The midnight wind and rain was the worst I'd ever seen. The threat of serious damage was real and closing in. The danger was no longer abstract, something you see on TV, happening to other people.

I prayed to God—yes, for safety, but mostly for the courage to live without possessions. I thought the wind might blow the roof away. It seemed a distinct likelihood. This was no time for bargaining with the divine. This was a moment to face the raging power of nature, the power of creation that an Almighty had fashioned and unleashed from the beginning of time, a fearful mystery and no point whitewashing its dangers. It was time to brace for the whirlwind and hope to get through it one way or another.

But when dreaded daybreak arrived, something unpredictable happened. The lashing winds and rain died down. The hurricane weakened and sputtered.

We were fortunate, this time—maybe not next time, and certainly not for all time. It's arrogant nonsense to assume violent disaster happens only to others. This delicate thing called normal life was never meant to be permanent. Someone is always in the path of destruction, and they deserve empathy and solidarity. Eventually the suffering touches everyone. It is well to remember those who are in terrible need this very moment and treat them as neighbors whether near or far. One day the rest of us, one by one, might taste that desperation.

After the storm ended, the power was out, so that night my wife and I came to the end of the ordeal in candlelight in our darkened living room. The effect was a kind of vespers service: sighs of relief provided the liturgy. Commitment to a clear-eyed realism about the risks of this life was our silent benediction.

No book that attempts to pursue any such notion as an undistorted God should go without a mention of natural disaster. Honesty demands it. Books about God, after a while, tend to give the impression of being on cozy terms with the divine mind. The existence of cataclysms is a rebuke to any tidy narrative, false uplift, or claim to understand the will of God. Life can change in an instant. The abyss and the things that give life somehow move together. The distance between shadow and light is too close to wish away.

When I step up to the communion rail, I don't want to forget any of this. The life affirmations of the communion meal should not be prettified or removed from all memory of danger or the victims of danger. The Eucharistic prayers and meal are themselves forged from the most unpromising circumstances. A looming violence and dread of death defined that original Last Supper: Jesus was executed the next day. At that dinner gathering with his disciples and friends he called on a divine power that, later that night in the garden, would make him tremble and sweat with a sense of abandonment.

That power of the Creator, destructive and redemptive, is what Jesus faced on the cross: a bleak non-answer, forsakenness, then in the fullness of time the blinding dawn of resurrection. The bread and wine of a regular worship service—even such small portions—capture that disorder. Eucharist houses that storm. It harnesses it.

That day at the communion rail, getting skipped, I beheld God's power at a new angle. A storm broke in my head. Then before long it was stilled. Mysterious power—destructive, redemptive, the sort that can generate a coastal hurricane or start a world-changing course of truth—was transfigured into a meal. "Eat my flesh" and "drink my blood," images of a horror film, are turned into a peaceable invitation to nourishment and celebration. At communion the partaker summons a divine force, or moves closer to it, that is stronger than the storm. It could flatten us there on the spot. Yet it channels itself into welcome and forgiveness. This power commands and demands respect.

"On the whole, I do not find Christians, outside of the catacombs, sufficiently sensible of conditions," Annie Dillard once wrote. "Does anyone have the foggiest idea what sort of power we so blithely invoke? Or, as I suspect, does no one believe a word of it? The churches are children playing on the floor with their chemistry sets, mixing up a batch of TNT to kill a Sunday morning. It is madness to wear ladies' straw hats and velvet hats to church; we should all be wearing crash helmets."[1]

I don't take Dillard's words to be mere whimsy. A great force convulses through the world, barely controllable, a dynamic of wind and electrons and spirit, at turns visible and invisible, an echo of some inconceivable beginning, powerful enough to sustain life, inspire Haydn and Michelangelo and missionary doctors, forge liturgies and sanctuaries, and assemble deadly weather.

Dozens of storm references show up in the Bible, and it's interesting what commentators do with them. Most famously for Christians, Jesus quiets the storm in Matthew 8 after getting caught in a squall on the lake with his disciple companions. It's customary to take this scene as symbolic of Jesus's power over nature. But I'm not interested in symbols. A super storm bearing down in real time on real earth is not primarily symbolic to people in its path.

A passage from First Kings gives a clue to these matters:

> The LORD said, "Go out and stand at the mountain before
> the LORD. The LORD is passing by." A very strong wind
> tore through the mountains and broke apart the stones
> before the Lord. But the LORD wasn't in the wind. After the
> wind, there was an earthquake. But the LORD wasn't in the
> earthquake. After the earthquake, there was a fire. But the
> LORD wasn't in the fire. After the fire, there was a sound.
> Thin. Quiet. When Elijah heard it, he wrapped his face in
> his coat. He went out and stood at the cave's entrance. A
> voice came to him and said, "Why are you here, Elijah?"[2]

Taking a moment's meditation during the super storm, unable to escape the roar, I soon felt a weird, rare freedom. Earlier, the dread wanted to pin me down and smother me. Now a different sort of internal motion was pushing ahead. In prayer I imagined God to be free of the engulfing whirlwind, separate from it and waiting, and I felt cause to move to that space of freedom.

Ever since, whenever I kneel at communion, I wonder at that same invisible presence, the one I call on as directly during the Eucharistic prayers as I did in the wind and rain. "God of all power, Ruler of the Universe," says the prayer in *The Book of Common Prayer*, "you are worthy of glory and praise. At your command all things came to be: the vast expanse of interstellar space, galaxies, suns, the planets in their courses, and this fragile earth, our island home."[3] *Fragile*—they got that right.

So, in a storm, or at the communion rail, there's no time for symbolism. I keep my eyes open. I am never more willing to be literal than at communion, where the liturgy declares that God's property is always to have mercy, and throngs of angels stand before the divine presence day and night, and heaven and earth are full of God's glory.

Flannery O'Connor famously said: if the Eucharist isn't real, if it's just a symbol, then to hell with it.[4] To her it was the center of existence, the space from which one rides out the staggering convulsions of time. I take her to mean that the Creator of all power who delivered vast interstellar space can also curate the details of a bit of bread and wine, using that power to transform a life. If it's just a clever symbol, then forget it. Grace happens, but it can only happen in the real world among its anguished details and materials.

The only catch that day when we corrected the little communion misunderstanding was this: I took the elements alone, not with others. The others had already had theirs. I was catching up. The pre-Eucharistic prayers caution worshipers to be reconciled with other people before going up there. This has always required a personal seat-of-the-pants judgment call, a little exercise in self-leniency. I justify my imperfect preparation for communion by hoping that the act itself will soften my pride and help me forgive. It also keeps me hoping that others will forgive me. By custom, when the Eucharistic meal is completed we look around and realize we just finished this mystery together. This experience, so private, is yet held in common. Full of communion elements and gospel memory, we must now move into the future unknown, commencing a pilgrimage into the open.

Whether one is kneeling in a stone chapel in sweet silence or raising a family in a world of pressurized distraction or hunkering down in 100 mile per hour winds, one condition is the same in each case: we have no clear grasp of the next turn, yet we're still capable of taking the next step in front of us, then the next, in a direction of good will, toward the light.

"The way of the pilgrim"—a phrase of scholar Richard Wentz—sounds just right. As he puts it, a pilgrim is a restless quester who is fueled by a certain mandate: he is not weighed down by nostalgia or ideology or materialism but is attentive to his "homeward-yearning journey," a move toward truth. This pilgrimage is no mere symbol. It's a description of the human situation. And it's something done with others.

> *Full of communion elements and gospel memory, we must now move into the future unknown, commencing a pilgrimage into the open.*

"The pilgrim knows that life is a matter of 'we,' not 'I,'" he writes. "It is a pilgrimage with neighbors, seen and unseen."[5]

What if there were no Eucharist or communion? What if faith's long pilgrimage never included such a liturgy? I suppose the gospel news of resurrection wouldn't be any different if there were no Last Supper and no communion meal of formalized remembrance of Jesus. But the report of Last Supper puts him squarely in history and in the path of the future, giving him specific density and weight. Without those specifications, he'd float weightlessly among the world's philosophical frolics, which are happy to minimize his pain or humanity or mission and turn him into a magician or chimera or life coach or something other than what his followers experienced in him. Without Eucharist, there'd be one less earthly meeting place with his memory, his expectations, and his spirit.

In the introduction I said the faith waits for us. Its promises and tenacity appear in different guises, as communion, meditation, action, kinship with another person's hunger, another's alienation. The faith is there to step up to and into. I step up to it at the railing, meeting the bread and wine. I hope to be a reliable partner to it, bring supplies from time to time, and invite other guests. The hope, the wavering vow, is to stay clear headed enough to carry that re freshment into the next few minutes and beyond, until this slight advantage of courage is tested once more in the next maelstrom, the next tomorrow, and I depend on grace again.

Yes, the clutter is still there. It's invincible—almost. An old impulse wants to cling to familiar formulas or resentments. Almost. The paths are there for circling back to the surprise of belief, which waits among the many hazards and shadows and beams of light.

NOTES

Introduction: A Decluttered Faith

1. Robert Lowell, "*Dies Irae*," in *History* (New York: Farrar, Straus, and Giroux, 1973), 74.

1. Elements of God

1. John Updike, "The Music School," in *The Music School: Short Stories* (New York: Fawcett World Library, 1967), 143.

4. Rebirth of God

1. Muriel Rukeyser, "The Speed of Darkness," in *Out of Silence: Selected Poems*, ed. Kate Daniels (Evanston, IL: TriQuarterly Books, 1992), 135.

2. Isaac Bashevis Singer, "Yes . . . ," *Esquire Magazine*, December 1974, 253–54.

3. Angelus Silesius, *The Book of Angelus Silesius*, trans. Frederick Franck (Santa Fe, NM: Bear & Co., 1985), 78. Also: "Christ could be born a thousand times in Galilee—but all in vain until He is born in me" (p. 107).

5. Rhythm of God

1. Bruce Cockburn, "When You Give It Away," *Breakfast in New Orleans . . . Dinner in Timbuktu,* High Romance Music Limited, 1999.

2. Living in the South, as I do, gives a person plenty of evidence of the great tensions between belief and society that can shape music in the first place. Jazz and blues—the South's great musical gifts to the world—sprung from

the moral catastrophes of slavery, poverty, and defeat. That such beauty was wrung from such violent suffering is a contradiction that only a world religion (Southern Christianity) or a great literature (William Faulkner, Flannery O'Connor, and gang) has the stamina to absorb. The kind of contradictions that break individuals to pieces can somehow be used or redeemed through beauty, giving itself back to people as a healing gift.

3. See George Steiner, *Real Presences* (Chicago: University of Chicago Press, 1989), 218.

4. The little book *The Music of Silence: Entering the Sacred Space of Monastic Experience*, by David Steindl-Rast, with Sharon Lebell (San Francisco: HarperSanFrancisco, 1995), makes a similar point about Gregorian chant: "The chant speaks to our hearts today because it is a universal call to enter the *now*: to stop, to listen, and to heed the message of *this* moment. It speaks to the monk in each of us, to our soul, which longs for peace and connection to an ultimate source of meaning and value" (p. 5).

7. Motion of God

1. Stephen Prothero, introduction to *The Best Spiritual Writing 2013*, ed. Philip Zaleski (New York: Penguin, 2013), xvii.

2. Martin Amis, *The Paris Review Interviews, III* (New York: Picador, 2008), 345.

3. Henry David Thoreau, *The Essays of Henry D. Thoreau*, ed. Lewis Hyde (New York: North Point Press, 2002), 177.

4. John McQuiston II, *Always We Begin Again: The Benedictine Way of Living* (Harrisburg, PA: Morehouse, 1996), 19–20. He writes: "It is for us to train our hearts to live in grace, to sacrifice our self-centered desires, to find the peace without want without seeking it for ourselves, and when we fail, to begin again each day" (pp. 21–22).

8. Miracle of God

1. See Joseph Brodsky, "25.XII.1993," in *Nativity Poems* (New York: Farrar, Straus, and Giroux, 2001), 95.

2. Scholar C. F. D. Moule believes the healings of Jesus were not miraculous at all but simply natural events that happened because Jesus the healer per-

fectly embodied the will of God and the recipient fully trusted God. They are not miracles but acts of power, signs that the sovereignty of God—the alignment of the will of God and people's trust in God—is, fitfully, at hand. See C. F. D. Moule, *The Gospel According to Mark: Cambridge Bible Commentary* (Cambridge, U.K.: Cambridge University Press, 1965), 15–16.

3. William H. Gass, *Life Sentences: Literary Judgments and Accounts* (New York: Knopf, 2012), 3.

10. Timetable of God

1. Mark 13:31-32.

2. My home region of the country—the "crossroads," or states that reside at that borderland between the old Confederate South and the frontier West—was always especially rife with conflict. Slavery versus abolition, traditionalist versus modernist, populist versus elitist, countryside versus city, Old West versus Old South, Baptist versus charismatic versus Catholic, government versus business, federalism versus armed individualism—these produced a showdown mentality, a regional habit of agitated thinking that has since spread to become a national style. Arguments about Armageddon were a natural fit. The crossroads states are Louisiana, Oklahoma, Texas, Arkansas, and Missouri. See William Lindsey and Mark Silk, eds., *Religion & Public Life in the Southern Crossroads* (Walnut Creek, CA: AltaMira Press, 2004). With essays and stats offered by seven scholar-contributors, it describes this fateful sectional sensibility in ways overlooked before.

3. Henri Frankfort et al., *The Intellectual Adventure of Ancient Man* (Chicago: University of Chicago Press, 1946), 46.

4. Thomas Merton, audiotape address, 1965, cited in Marcus Borg, *The Heart of Christianity: Rediscovering a Life of Faith* (New York: HarperSanFrancisco, 2003), 155.

5. Ralph Waldo Emerson, *Emerson in His Journals*, ed. Joel Porte (Cambridge, MA: Harvard University Press, 1982), 131.

11. Image of God

1. Joshua ben Levi, quoted in Byron Sherwin, *Jewish Ethics for the Twenty-First Century: Living in the Image of God* (Syracuse, NY: Syracuse University Press, 2000), 1.

2. Leon R. Kass, *The Beginning of Wisdom: Reading Genesis* (New York: Free Press, 2003), 39.

3. John 14:7.

4. John 14:11.

5. John 15:4-5.

6. William Blake, "The Divine Image," in *Norton Anthology of English Literature*, vol. 2, 4th ed., ed. M. H. Abrams (New York: W. W. Norton), 34.

7. Will Campbell, *Brother to a Dragonfly* (New York: Continuum, 2000), 220.

12. Seasons of God

1. J. Philip Newell, *Celtic Benediction: Morning and Night Prayer* (Grand Rapids, MI: Eerdmans, 2000), 59. In the preface he says: "Celtic spirituality is marked by the belief that what is deepest in us is the image of God. Sin has distorted and obscured that image but not erased it. The Mediterranean tradition, on the other hand, in its doctrine of original sin has taught that what is deepest in us is our sinfulness. This has given rise to a tendency to define ourselves in terms of the ugliness of our failings instead of the beauty of our origins."

2. William Shakespeare, Sonnet 65, in *The Sonnets* (New York: Penguin Group, 2001), 68.

13. Speech of God

1. Ecclesiastes 5:2.

2. Ecclesiastes 12:13.

3. John 21:9-17.

14. Endurance of God

1. Rowan Williams, *Ponder These Things: Praying with Icons of the Virgin* (Brewster, MA: Paraclete Press, 2012), xvii. He continues: "We, watching and waiting for Christ to come more fully to birth in us, are waiting for our lives to become 'iconic,' to show in their colour and line and movement how God acts, Christlike, in us."

2. Albert Schweitzer, *The Quest for the Historical Jesus*, ed. John Bowden (Norwich, UK: SCM Press, 2000), 487.

15. Geography of God

1. See Paul Froese and Christopher Bader, *America's Four Gods: What We Say about God—and What That Says about Us* (New York: Oxford University Press, 2010).

2. Gustav Janouch, *Conversations with Kafka*, introduction by Francine Prose (New York: New Directions, 2012), 6.

16. Vigil of God

1. D. H. Lawrence, "Books," in *Phoenix: The Posthumous Papers of D. H. Lawrence*, ed. Edward D. McDonald (New York: Viking Press, 1936), 734.

17. Fear of God

1. See Wade Clark Roof, *Spiritual Marketplace: Baby Boomers and the Remaking of American Religion* (Princeton, NJ: Princeton University Press, 1999), 48ff.

2. This is happening in a media-saturated climate that demonizes the opposition and keeps the world addicted to conflict and exaggeration. Americans don't trust each other like they did a generation ago. In 1960, 60 percent of Americans said they could trust most people. By 2006, that number had fallen to 32 percent, the lowest ever, says Farhad Manjoo in his book *True Enough: Learning to Live in a Post-Fact Society* (Hoboken, NJ: Wiley & Sons, 2008), 223.

3. Blind Willie Johnson (1897–1945) recorded the song in 1930. Many others have performed it since, including Bruce Cockburn on his record *Nothing but a Burning Light* (1991).

4. Earl Shorris, *The Politics of Heaven: America in Fearful Times* (New York: W. W. Norton, 2007), 343.

5. Ibid.

6. Phyllis Trible, "Authority of the Bible," in *The New Interpreter's Study Bible: New Revised Standard Version with the Apocrypha* (Nashville: Abingdon Press, 2003), 2252. She adds: "For certain, the authority of the Bible does not rest on its being a seamless document with a homogeneous or monolithic meaning. To the contrary, conflicting voices keep open meanings and appropriations. Despite efforts by editors, canonizers, and

interpreters, no one person or group controls the meanings of the content. Biblical authority embraces the authority of struggle and difference; the authority of struggle and difference undergirds biblical authority" (p. 2253).

7. "Fear, Awe, Dread," by R. Gregor Smith in *A Theological Word Book of the Bible*, ed. Alan Richardson (New York: MacMillan, 1950), 81.

8. Richard Howard, cited in *God Knows My Heart* by Christine Wicker (New York: St. Martin's Press, 1999), 175.

9. Proverbs 30:7-9.

18. Power of God

1. Annie Dillard, *Teaching a Stone to Talk: Expeditions and Encounters* (New York: Harper & Row, 1982), 40.

2. 1 Kings 19:11-13.

3. *The Book of Common Prayer*, from Eucharistic Prayer C (New York: Seabury Press, 1979), 370.

4. Flannery O'Connor, from a letter dated December 16, 1955, in *Flannery O'Connor: Collected Works* (New York: Library of America, 1988), 977.

5. Richard Wentz, *Why Do People Do Bad Things in the Name of Religion?* (Macon, GA: Mercer University, 1987). He writes: "The pilgrim simply realizes what is true for all of us: we are restless beings because we transcend the world in which we exist. 'Our hearts are restless,' said St. Augustine, 'until they find their rest in thee.' The pilgrim disciplines his homelessness. He works at the Quest, the 'homeward-yearning,' and tries to control his restlessness. . . . We can confess the violence that is in us, that we share with the most reprehensible of terrorists. We can be prepared to move lightly and quickly, to deny the modern passion for power and property. . . . At the heart of the pilgrim's way is the knowledge that he is free. He is bound to no system. He has nothing to defend and lives only to care for everything that is" (pp. 82–83).

READER'S GUIDE
& CONVERSATION TOOLS

INTRODUCTION: A DECLUTTERED FAITH

I was eager to pursue, move closer to, some divine impulse at the base of it all, some spark of permanence that survives the onslaughts of spiritual fashion and controversy.

◆ The author admits his "religious receptors are just average." How do you sharpen those religious receptors and what kind of difference would that make?

◆ "In-breakings happen." What are the events and turbulences that test the fabric of the familiar for you? List several of those. How have they become reminders of God, evidence of a divine persistence, the shadow and motion of the Creator?

◆ "We are all seeking a way out from under the chaos. What's exciting is the endeavor of cutting a path out of it, by circling

back to those strangely powerful, enduring materials of faith."
What are those enduring materials of faith in your own life?

1. ELEMENTS OF GOD: WINE OF ASTONISHMENT

The prayers had been said, and now it was time to approach the rail. Good—I was glad just to get up, get moving, and walk toward the altar, a sanctified stroll to escape the mental fog.

I waited on bent knees like so many times before. The minister leaned over to each person in turn, dispensing the little beige rounded wafers, heading closer, closer.

She skipped me.

My face froze. What just happened? Cool reason horned in: she's out of wafers, I thought. But no. She continued on to the others. I could see plenty of wafers in her hand.

◆ During key meaningful moments or rituals, perhaps we have been bypassed, overlooked, or ignored. Sometimes those moments have affected us deeply. Why is that so devastating? If you recall such moments in your life, why does it feel like excommunication? And have you ever been brave enough to question that and—at least from your end—take a step to changing that dynamic, saying, "Hey, you skipped me up there," and making it right?

◆ What are the ways that you face (or don't face) your decision to make it right when you have been left out?

2. LARGESSE OF GOD: BEYOND IBELIEF

Some years ago I met a woman who took an especially keen interest in spiritual questions: What's the strangest religion I ever heard of, she asked me. How can anyone know which one is true? Big themes. It sounded like she was wrestling with a decision to go to seminary. Finally she told me what was really on her mind.
"I want to start my own religion," she declared.

◆ Admit it, you've sometimes wanted to start your own religion. Maybe you haven't found the church, the tradition you hoped to find. Maybe you felt like the church has lost touch with you as a spiritual seeker. What are the questions that you think a faith or faith practice needs to answer, address, or keep asking in order to avoid redundancy, slow motion, lethargic worship?

◆ Somehow, the author writes, the coordinates of religion and belief—transformation, ethics, testimony, discipleship, divine presence—got knocked askew. The vocabulary lost traction. Where are the places you are seeking traction? Where are you seeing a rich vocabulary that still holds meaning? Where are you seeing strong ethics? Where is testimony a significant ethical witness?

3. SON OF GOD: GO CRAZY

We're a culture of competing Christs, a world of jostling Jesuses. Everyone claims a user-friendly redeemer to shore up

151

a particular vision of holiness or political prejudice. It's embar-
rassing. Who is Jesus? I could name thirty different Jesuses right
now—or is it three hundred? Or three hundred million?

◆ The author lists seven "Jesuses." Which one have you intentionally claimed, unintentionally claimed, or intentionally not
claimed?

> • Free-market Messiah
> • Peace-and-Justice Jesus
> • Silence of the Lamb (of God)
> • Rapturous redeemer
> • Self-help holy man
> • Childhood Christ
> • Gnostic prankster

◆ "I read the Gospel to keep from going crazy," the author writes.
What do you read, what keeps you returning to true faith, what
keeps Jesus on a line of sight? Where do you see the Word
made flesh and flesh made Word?

4. REBIRTH OF GOD: VERB AND REVERB

I've since wondered at his bristling assumptions about faith and
damnation and how quickly our little exchange turned into an arid
canyon of broken communication between two ostensible believers.

He had his story of salvation, and he was sticking with it. And
I have mine.

◆ We tend to put out stakes in the ground and make statements about our stories of salvation. Others have their stories and we have ours. And we're sticking to our story. When we do, our communication with others gets broken. When have you been so sure your version of faith was the right one that the conversation was over before it began? When have you met someone who took the risk of not being right in order to create a bridge in talking about faith?

◆ Respond to this statement by the author: That's a tragedy of modern Christianity—the long-nurtured, closely guarded sectarian divisions between believers over the credentials of one's conversion, even the style of telling the story of one's redemption. But never mind. There are many ways to tell the tale, many ways through to the other side.

◆ The author quotes the Jewish writer Isaac Bashevis Singer: "God is a writer and we are both the heroes and the readers." It's rare to see a theology delivered in thirteen words. What other quotations have you read or heard that have shined a light on theology, delivering it up in 12 or 20 or 30 words?

5. RHYTHM OF GOD: MYSTERY TOUR

Life roared into the unknown: salvation a work in progress, never a sealed book. It sounded scary. But I sensed something providentially larger than ourselves was watching as we plotted the next move or blundered into it.

In other words, I was awakening to the existence of my own soul, which was powerfully radiating, registering the new conditions. I had to face its exacting presence.

◆ The author writes about a profound early meeting with a poly-rhythmic beat and global sound in a Beatles tune. Something shifts in him and challenges the way he perceives his soul. When has music radiated so powerfully that you registered something new about your soul, your faith, your life?

◆ What are some of the soundtrack songs of your life—songs that have summoned something startling, opened breathing space, provided rest or defiance or regeneration?

◆ The author has a list of musicians at the end of the chapter. What are your sacred sonic encounters? What songs keep the soul's chapel hospitable, the doors open?

6. STORY OF GOD: REWRITING THE DARKNESS

Dad's absence presented itself now as a constant thought. His memory, my only link to him, has moved to the foreground since his death: a new presence. Absent, yet present. Is that just a clever paradox?

◆ We've all faced a long day, a long night, a sense of loss, absence, desperation. A sojourn. What have been your absences, those messengers from the void? What have they shown you? What have you observed? What has remained inexplicable and yet created something different in you?

◆ There are two stories, the author writes, the nihilism story—shards flashing out from the chaos—and the God story—bold lettering traced on the scroll of darkness. Do you agree that these are the two stories at stake when we are facing an abyss, reckoning with what comes after this life?

7. MOTION OF GOD: WALK THIS WAY

The treks of the patriarchs, the wanderings of the prophets, the momentum of the Jesus movement—walk speed was the mode of steady-spreading monotheism. For fifty years I've harbored a first-century fantasy: I should be walking to church and lots of other places, too.

◆ What are the ways you slow the pace so that you can pay attention to street-level life, to oak trees and bus stops and the Sunday paper?

◆ The author describes seeing Orthodox Jews walking to the synagogue from all over the neighborhood. And called it a scene of unplugged holiness. Can you recall such sacred scenes in your life? If you were to create intentional, unplugged holiness, what would that look like? And how can you begin the steps to unplugging and to holiness?

8. MIRACLE OF GOD: TRUE AND FALSE

The subject of miracles is a wild ride and, for a writer about religion, a professional dilemma. I've seen plenty of stage miracles. I can't say I was moved by any of them. Either they looked faked or they glorified the performer. Even the impressive ones left questions. What is the point of this? Should faith depend on these miracles? Should they be a test of belief? Do they express the presence of God? Do they distort the intentions of God? Perhaps they were signs of grace that were denied to me. Or maybe they were lost on me because I wasn't looking for them to happen.

◆ Why does the author say that the miraculous is a hazardous subject? Why is it hard to find the right distance on it? The right gaze?

◆ Are you a miracles skeptic? In what ways are you open to testimony, to their possibility, but not hemmed in by one cherished interpretation of events or a tyrannical reading of scripture or life that bullies people into a deep-dish doctrinal stance?

◆ There's only one miracle that counts, claims the author. Why is that the central *miracle?*

9. HOUSE OF GOD: SITUATION ROOM

Much of the time it's nearly impossible to look at church and see it aright, see it for what it is: a chamber where the normal laws of gravity are suspended. It's a crucible where sacred and profane jostle and try to make peace. It's a ragtag encampment of wanderers throwing their future in with a juggernaut of the divine. Take away the parking lot and the video screen and microphone, and the place is no different from a dusty Christian catacomb of year 150 CE: a beleaguered, shuffling miracle.

◆ When have you been in a sacred space and somehow the rules were broken, something unexpected made the space a little different, awkward? Did you ask questions, like the author, when he exchanged the peace in church and was asked for money? Could you have handled it differently? Did you cave in to sentimental guilt? Could you have been more generous? Did you feel like you failed a test? What kind of test was it?

◆ Where have you witnessed the upside-down world that is church, a place that engages you but more often exposes you?

◆ Churches disagree on a thousand points of theology or worship or politics. What do you believe they share that is more important than any difference?

10. TIMETABLE OF GOD: MINISTRY OF FEAR

As it turns out, the only impressive thing about the end-time stuff, century after century, is its 100-percent failure rate. Yet the discredited prognosticators keep coming back. They understand the power of fear to worm its way into our psyches and obliterate trust in a 3,500-year-old biblical message that says God made creation and said it was good.

◆ In which ways have you witnessed the power of fear used by religion—the threat of hell, the dangling promise of the end times—to distort a profound message?

◆ So much of religion's time, including our own, can be taken up by overheated end-of-days soap operas. The author's call is to an incarnational theology, a tour of the world where the elements of the creation are sacramental signs, God's fingerprints. What kind of change would living with that incarnational heart and motion mean for your life?

11. IMAGE OF GOD: ENTOURAGE

Imagine this, if you dare: whenever a human being walks past you, a posse of angels is right there hard at work, silently yet forcefully announcing, "Behold, the image of God!"

◆ The image of God is a revolutionary idea with ramifications for interpersonal relations, art, and politics. What does it mean that this could be—ought to be—a starting point for religious common ground?

◆ Where have you witnessed dividing lines in religion melting away? What do you believe caused that?

◆ How does a line like this one by the author change how you might see an enemy, a friend, a co-worker: If the image of God is really imprinted on each person, then I can't accept it for myself and deny it in someone else.

12. SEASONS OF GOD: EARTH TONES

It's not a matter of condemning this new world. It's our world—vivid, mesmerizing, indispensable, fast. But there is power in naming what's challenging or peculiar about it, what it loses or disregards or retards. There's a need to take back our own power from the sleepless demanding stream of data. By reconnecting with the natural world—in the sharp glint of stone, fire, tree—the intuitions of the five senses bloom again.

◆ The author writes about reconnecting with the natural world, its associations and surfaces, and his own sense of homecoming when he touches a stone cross in Iona. What are some of the re-connectors of the natural world for you? What associations do you make, what history does it bring, what wonder and reflection took place for you? Is it like a homecoming for you?

◆ What does honoring both a linear sense of time and also a cyclical view of nature time mean? How does that change or preserve a mindful respect for creation?

13. SPEECH OF GOD: SILENT PARTNER

Reports occasionally come out about pilgrims or travelers who go temporarily unhinged in Jerusalem, burning with biblical utterance, stripping off their clothes, declaring themselves to be God's next prophet or messiah announcing the end of time. They are reacting to the severities of the city's narrow lanes, the succession of centuries and conflicts. It gets to be too much to digest in mind and soul. Some people blow a fuse: it's called the Jerusalem Syndrome. They usually recover with some therapy, or simply by leaving the high-octane scene and going back home.

◆ Impatience, the author writes, is an underestimated force in religious history. When the divine silence refuses to break, we fill it ourselves. What are the ways that you have filled in—on a small scale or large—that divine silence?

◆ How can the silence of God and the presence of God become the same thing, as the author suggests? Have you ever experienced that?

14. ENDURANCE OF GOD: KNOWN UNKNOWN

Yet the image of Jesus is there to keep me circling back to first principles—scripture, sacraments, memory, hope, action—despite the noise machine, despite tumultuous past and uncer-

tain future. Conjuring the stained-glass silent Jesus with the flock of sheep, I feel a rebuke. I get the lingering impression that the figure in the glass panel isn't particularly impressed by any thumbnail argument of cultural decline or doctrinal triumphalism or self-pity. He's quite literally unmoved, as if underwhelmed by it all. The day's many psychodramas aren't as awesome as we think. The baseline of human nature didn't change after Woodstock, Vietnam, Watergate, Reaganomics, terrorism, globalization, climate change, and whatever was hot this morning in social media. The condition of the invisible God hasn't changed either.

◆ What are the images of Jesus that linger for you, despite tumultuous past and uncertain future?

◆ Grandeur, reverence, beauty, and silence are not the marks of some musty worship style that the 1960s swept away. Those things are a fixed condition of human need across the ages. Without them, the author writes, I wither and flatten. What are other markers of a fixed condition of human need across the ages?

15. GEOGRAPHY OF GOD: GOING PLACES

Everybody knows places that are infused with a religious mood. Specific theologies attend landscapes. There is such a thing as spiritual geography.

◆ What are places you know that are infused with a spiritual or religious mood?

◆ The author suggests that landscape can influence or shape one's image of God. What is your image of God, and why? Does it conflict with other well-known divine images?

16. VIGIL OF GOD: MONASTERY CONFIDENTIAL

The gospel adventure toward God continues. The ark floating on the blind, roaring sea still carries the freight of truth-seeking, peacemaking, and incarnation toward God. A monastery visit confirms it. So does the work of a million churches.

◆ Despite early hesitation, the author decides to write a "letter to God" during a visit to a monastery. It becomes a form of self-discovery and prayer. Have you ever communicated to God in this way? What would your letter say?

◆ After his monastery visit, the author is determined to find commitment and serenity in daily life in order to continue the "venture toward God." How do you launch your own venture toward God? How do you keep the momentum going? What thoughts or practices do you take on the journey?

17. FEAR OF GOD: BURNING LIGHT

A lot of exasperated people have simply given up on religion. They made a shift. They now get their moral passion from politics instead. . . . Many such people used to connect with congregational life, where they discovered a personal place in a providential universe and a specific duty to the Golden Rule. Healthy religion inspired personal restraint, business integrity, and public truthfulness. People believed God was watching.

◆ A lot of people these days are more passionate about politics than discipleship and faith, the author says. Ideology has succeeded in dividing us, and religion has failed to unite us. Can Christian faith be a force of healing across political and economic lines?

◆ The Bible is a living, provocative document, the author says. Its authority is in the turbulence and wonder it still stirs. Is that your experience of reading scripture? How does the Bible fit in your life? What does it mean to say the Bible is true?

18. POWER OF GOD: EUCHARIST REVISITED

Books about God, after a while, tend to give the impression of being on cozy terms with the divine mind. The existence of cataclysms is a rebuke to any tidy narrative, false uplift, or claim to understand the will of God. Life can change in an instant. The

163

abyss and the things that give life somehow move together. The distance between shadow and light is too close to wish away.

When I step up to the communion rail, I don't want to forget any of this.

◆ What does the power and sovereignty of God mean to you? Does it include control of the weather?

◆ The author quotes the phrase the "way of the pilgrim" as a useful metaphor—the pilgrim travels light, focuses on the goal of truth, and makes the sojourn with others. Is the odyssey of faith a private or a communal undertaking? Does one follow from the other?

MEET THE AUTHOR.
Read about the Book.

You've been writing about faith both as a reporter and a columnist, now, for thirty years. When did your passion for writing about/exploring faith begin for you?

I was a churchgoing kid, but I always had questions about why the worship service was structured the way it was, why we prayed or sang what we did, and why the world was full of very different, conflicting religious expressions and how they compared. I sensed a long history of faith playing out—a long conversation with God. But we didn't talk about that. My questions grew.

Social change was grinding away at every turn. Christian tradition and contemporary society looked to be on a collision course. Or were they influencing each other? Or does one dominate for a while, then the other pushes back and gets momentum? Or was God at work through it all? I got interested in that—the interplay of religious claims and cultural change. I wondered what truths are permanent amid all the passing noise and crises.

So I helplessly became a writer. The compulsion started early. I was keeping detailed journals of family vacations at age eleven or so and later got on the high school newspaper. In college I did a journalism degree, then in graduate school a religious studies degree. I wanted to combine the writing and the spiritual endeavor somehow—try to get it down on the page and find order there.

As an occupation, writing about religion was a way to stay in touch daily with these questions and get to know people—ministers, artists, activists, philosophers, skeptics, poets—who were working out answers. I got to sift through them. I got in at a good time, the 1980s, when public religion was asserting itself in politics, the culture wars, street protests, the arts. Today, the publication I edit, *Reflections* journal at Yale Divinity School, does something similar. It examines how belief and ethics can illuminate and critique current affairs. The aim is to extend the school's mission of engaging faith and intellect to prepare leaders for church and world.

In the book you often structure chapters at the intersection of a moment—a meeting, an event—and find a spiritual connecting point. Is that an intentional decision?

Matters of faith don't unfold in a vacuum. Spiritual struggle and transformation happen in the gritty paradoxes of the moment, or not at all. Prayer happens despite the laws of gravity. Reconciliation defies all predictions. It's an incarnational idea: spirit carries somehow on the vexations of the physical world. That's how witnesses experienced Jesus—an intersection of earth and heaven, dust and transcendence.

It happened back then, it happens now, this Christian idea that the desperate material world is where the work of God gets done. I'm not a big fan of religious rhetoric that soars into realms of purity, going on as if suffering or war or mental illness or gravity doesn't exist. And the nonreligious attitude isn't adequate either if it assumes beauty and compassion are just a matter of molecules or luck or folly. I think that's naïve. And boring. Surely the point of life is more ambitious than that.

These connections between belief and world are paradoxical. But writers like paradox. It gives them more to sort out and write about. At the intersection of spirit and matter, writer tools like attention, patience, vigilance, and a bit of modesty are all useful. Those also happen to be spiritual attitudes.

In this book you write about people, churches, or political factions co-opting faith that claim their version of Jesus as the "real" Jesus. Your book, though, explores something that moves past those camps and schisms. How did such a beautiful book arise despite all that distraction and noise?

Thank you for that, but I didn't know where the book was going at first, because I was just trying to get to the bottom of a personal fascination or exasperation about why there are so many fragmented versions of Jesus out there. As an observer I was noticing a lot of self-serving editions of Christ. They often contradicted. No one seemed to be embarrassed by that!

So I tried at least to name some distorted views in order to demystify their power. Then I needed to face the gospel picture itself, which is a Jesus of many arguments and moods. He resists our oversimplifications and agendas. I found freedom in pursuing that. I didn't have to keep up anymore with all the wearying splinters and counterclaims. The noise started to fall away.

Frequently you write about scripture—that seems to be foundational in your writing. And yet, your writing quietly assumes that groundwork rather than quoting scripture throughout. What role does scripture play in your life of faith and in this book?

I can feel the Bible's shadow whether I'm reading it or not. Its stories embrace everything, claiming to account for the creation of every leaf, every person and galaxy. I'm interested in the ways we react to that—whether we accept it, deny it, distort it, wrestle hard with it, try to make it true in daily life.

The public career of the Bible, its stamina across history, is compelling. It seems to wait, silently, patiently, for the next person to reach for it and discover what's in there. Despite all the naysayers, it endures. Its survival and authority says: This book, this collection of books and stories told and retold, would not exist unless something, some inconceivable force or elemental presence, had sparked its writers, compilers, and editors. In short: they didn't make it all up. The stories of Abraham and Noah, the difficult ethics of Amos and Jeremiah, the traumas of Job—how strange and fierce they are. Why would anyone bother to make them up?

Same with the New Testament, which is centered on the figure of Jesus and how he was transformed and how he transfigured those he knew.

We can haggle about the Bible's details and interpretations, but it outlasts all that. "It's nothing but a burning light," the old blues song says. So maybe it's like a blinding supernova whose origins are impossible to trace: it fills the sky, unwavering, unblinking. I take it to be the great unwieldy poem of the human predicament and potential. It seems to carry a secret about itself, as poet Richard Howard once wrote, a secret for each reader, each time.

Is your book a call to prepare the faith for the future or a return to an ancient way?

There's always a scrimmage going on between the past and the future, a competition between images about the faith. Is Christian belief a rock and bulwark, unchanged and preserved for two thousand years? Or is it a roaring wind that pushes into the future, remaking everything it touches, not looking back, letting the dead bury their own dead?

Lately I've been thinking of the image of church as a firewall. No matter what convulsive change it always faces, it will find a way to resist the bullying of ideology and the corrosions of hopelessness. The firewall against destruction is built of communion bread and wine, the waters of baptism, scripture reading, prayer, song, human touch, eye contact, hospitality. Every new generation discovers these core things in its own way.

What message or challenge do you hope the reader will leave your book with?

I hope the book captures various moments—quirky or unexpected, I hope—that reveal a fresh way to pursue the divine despite the latest noise and clutter.

There's a lot of anger and mistrust these days: political, economic, regional. Religion too often is used to give people a sanctified reason for ideological divisions. How strange that all this American belief in God hasn't really softened trends of mistrust and income inequality and militarism and loneliness. I thought Christianity and biblical religion—Ten Commandments, Sermon on the Mount, the prophets' call to justice and mercy, the news of Resurrection—were supposed to trump political resentment and hatred.

I mention the poetry of belief in the book. To me poetry can awaken senses. Art and creativity can move us to new positions, more conciliatory ones, and I think the gospel is art in that sense: it reimagines our view of the world. But that's scary because it means moving away from comfortable, complacent ideologies. Seething tribal politics is very lucrative right now. It's an impressive money-making racket. It won't hesitate to use religion to do its dirty work. I like the thought that the gospel is a scandal to such thinking. The gospel shames it. That idea is lurking behind the book.

Your book is about reclaiming faith from the cultural clutter. What are some simple things your readers can do to intentionally reclaim or recognize that divine spark in their every day lives?

Become skeptical about the noise, for one thing. Skepticism usually means doubt about God and belief, but I think we can bring a spirit of skepticism to the conventional wisdom—today's uncontested consumerism, ego entitlement, nonstop media, ecological poisoning. I think we need to question the things that push in on us and take away our confidence and health and inner spaces. Gospel values cultivate a person's inner strength. They give courage for making one's way in the world and loving and improving the world. Prayer and worship and visiting prisons become forms of dissent. But they hardly have a fighting chance if people don't defy the competing noise.

I once made a list of things that might get at that. My list-making is better than my getting out there to do it. I'm still working on that.

- Help a neighbor for no reason.
- Fast for a day and give away the money you would have spent on food.
- Memorize the Ten Commandments.
- "Do not avoid the eyes of the homeless." (says writer Michael Ventura)
- Play music you used to dance to.
- Forgive an enemy (and a friend).

- Volunteer.
- Visit a retreat center.
- Learn all the books of the Bible.
- Read Martin Luther King's speeches.
- Say grace.
- Walk a labyrinth.
- "Simplify, simplify." (Thoreau)
- Write down your reasons for believing.
- Find a peaceful window view.
- Sit still for seventy-four minutes and listen to Beethoven's Ninth Symphony.
- Be accountable to somebody.
- Avoid email on the Sabbath.
- Know where your food comes from and how it's grown.
- Remember this statistic: 30,000 children die every day from poverty or malnutrition.
- "Practice resurrection." (says Wendell Berry)